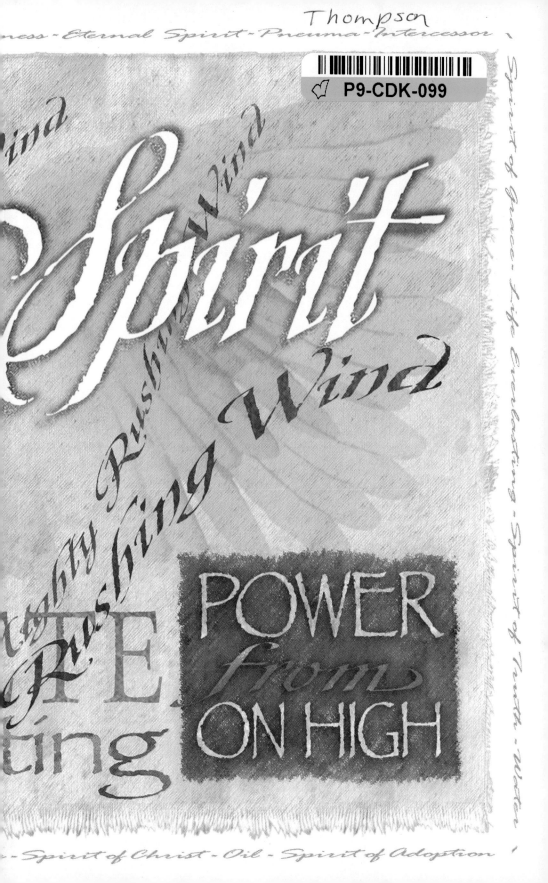

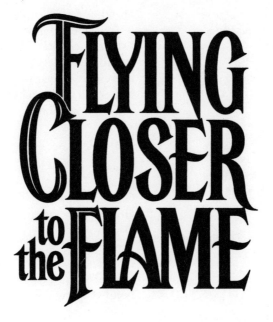

Publications by Charles R. Swindoll

Books

Come Before Winter
Compassion: Showing We Care in
  a Careless World
Dropping Your Guard
Encourage Me
For Those Who Hurt
The Grace Awakening
Growing Deep in the Christian
  Life
Growing Strong in the Seasons of
  Life
Growing Wise in Family Life
Hand Me Another Brick
Improving Your Serve
Killing Giants, Pulling Thorns
Laugh Again
Leadership: Influence That Inspires
Living Above the Level of
  Mediocrity
Living Beyond the Daily Grind,
  Books 1 and 2
Living on the Ragged Edge
Make Up Your Mind
The Quest for Character
Recovery: When Healing Takes
  Time
Rise and Shine
Sanctity of Life
Simple Faith
Standing Out
Starting Over
Strengthening Your Grip
Stress Fractures
Strike the Original Match
The Strong Family
Three Steps Forward, Two Steps
  Back
Victory: A Winning Game Plan for
  Life
You and Your Child

Minibooks

Abraham: A Model of Pioneer
  Faith
David: A Model of Pioneer
  Courage
Esther: A Model of Pioneer
  Independence
Moses: A Model of Pioneer Vision
Nehemiah: A Model of Pioneer
  Determination

Booklets

Anger
Attitudes
Commitment
Dealing with Defiance
Demonism
Destiny
Divorce
Eternal Security
Fun Is Contagious
God's Will
Hope
Impossibilities
Integrity
Leisure
The Lonely Whine of the Top Dog
Moral Purity
Our Mediator
Peace . . . in Spite of Panic
Prayer
Sensuality
Stress
Tongues
When Your Comfort Zone Gets
  the Squeeze
Woman

CHARLES R. SWINDOLL

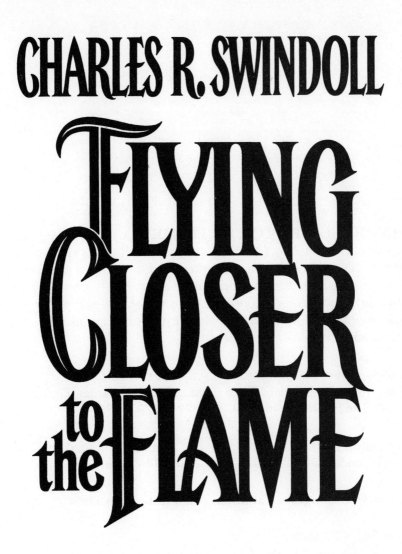

FLYING CLOSER to the FLAME

WORD PUBLISHING
Dallas•London•Vancouver•Melbourne

Unless otherwise indicated, all Scripture references are from The New American Standard Bible (NASB), © The Lockman Foundation 1960, 1962, 1963, 1968, 1971, 1972, 1973, 1975, 1977.

References marked AMP are from The Amplified Bible, copyright © 1965 Zondervan Publishing House. Used by permission.

Library of Congress Cataloging-in-Publication Data

Swindoll, Charles R.
    Flying closer to the flame : a passion for the Holy Spirit / Charles R. Swindoll.
      p. cm.
    Includes bibliographical references.
    ISBN 0-8499-1001-3
    1. Holy Spirit. 2. Spiritual life—Christianity. I. Title.
BT121.2.S955 1993
231'.3—dc20   93–5950
                                              CIP

34569   RRD   9 8 7 6 5 4 3 2 1

Printed in the United States of America.

It is with great admiration that I dedicate this book to my esteemed teacher, mentor, and, best of all, friend since 1959,

Dr. Donald K. Campbell

For forty years he has faithfully served his Lord on the faculty and in the administration of my alma mater, Dallas Theological Seminary, and since 1986 has served as the distinguished president of the school.

I thank my God upon every remembrance of this biblical scholar, outstanding theologian, and Christian gentleman, who, for as long as I have known him, has been flying close to the flame.

Contents

Acknowledgments

Books are like people. Each has its own personality. Furthermore, some require a great deal of assistance and support from a team of individuals, while others do not make such demands.

This volume falls into the latter category. Quietly and lovingly it was conceived in my mind. The thoughts and ideas that grew into pages and chapters emerged slowly, sometimes with great difficulty. I have been amazed at the things the Lord has brought into my life during the process of putting my thoughts into print. I have been through it! But this is not to say that the book was accomplished without anyone else's encouragement or assistance.

My closest friends at Word Publishing became aware of and mentioned the need for a book on the Holy Spirit about the time I began doing my research on the subject. We were all more than mildly concerned about much of what has been published and purchased on this subject over the past few years. As I read many of those works, I found myself disheartened to think that an ever-increasing number of people were reading (and believing!) things that lacked not only biblical support, but plain old common sense.

Through the urging of Byron Williamson at Word, I decided to turn my research into a volume that would provide trustworthy information and at the same time stretch the thinking of many superconservative Evangelicals without sounding like I had the final answer for the world. I also determined to remain positive and affirming wherever possible, rather than throw mud or point fingers at those with whom I disagree. I'm especially grateful that Byron, Kip Jordon, and David Moberg have been supportive as I have tried to walk the fine line of accuracy without sounding arrogant or angry. Doing that has taken time—a lot of time—which makes me indebted to all three for their patience.

As usual, Helen Peters, my extremely competent, longtime, ever-faithful executive assistant, has taken my rough draft of handwritten tablet pages and with ease and efficiency turned them into a manuscript any publisher would be envious to receive. Even as I was finishing this book, Helen decided to take early retirement, leaving her office at the church where we have worked together for more than twenty wonderful years. She will still assist me in my publishing ministry, but not having her on site on a daily basis has brought a huge feeling of loss to me personally. Since I began publishing back in the mid-1970s, Helen has been there to work her wonders and add her words of support. To say that I am thankful for her assistance is to state the obvious. If you find these pages helpful, much of the credit goes to her . . . as well as my editor, Judith Markham. They worked together, turning my original and primitive lines into meaningful and well-connected thoughts.

The congregation of the First Evangelical Free Church of Fullerton, California, also deserves my acknowledgments. As I hammered out my ideas in the study, the most natural place to communicate them was to this flock I have pastored since 1971. How encouraging they have been! Sunday after Sunday, as I would declare the fruit of my study, various ones would invariably challenge something I said, or ask for clarification, or simply thank me for going beyond the bounds of safety and taking the risk of originality while not altogether ignoring traditional boundaries.

Flying closer to the flame often required my leaving the comfort zone and being willing to be misunderstood. I am thankful that they never clipped my wings. It is because of their enthusiastic response that I felt the freedom to dare drawing closer and to declare the truth as I discovered and understood it.

So, here it is—a fresh and somewhat surprising series of thoughts on Him whom our Savior sent to be among us, to live within us, to work His will through us, to manifest His glory for us, and to reveal the truth to us. If this volume proves to be as helpful to you as the original thoughts and applications have been to me, we can both give our praise to Christ, who did not leave us "as orphans" but gave us "another Helper" to be with us forever (John 14:16, 18).

Introduction

This is a book about some of the intimate workings of the Holy Spirit. Unlike most books on the subject, you will find it personal, practical, and positive.

It is not primarily a theological workbook designed to analyze and criticize. There are enough of those. Neither is it a two-fisted, negative warning against all the errors floating around and among the ranks of Christians. Again, others have already done that. I have no interest in entering the arena of a debate that was going on long before I was born and will continue long after I'm gone.

My great hope in these pages is to step away from the heat of theological battle and move quietly and closely to the One who has been sent alongside to help. He longs to empower us with His dynamic presence, change our attitudes, warm our hearts, show us how and where to walk, comfort us in our struggles and our sorrows, strengthen us in the weak and fragile places of our lives, and literally revolutionize our pilgrimage from this planet to paradise.

Candidly, this is a book for the heart much more than for the head. I'm not saying you won't need to think or approach these subjects intelligently, but this is not an exhaustive theological treatment of the person and work of the Holy Spirit. Please keep that in mind. My goal, however, is to have you travel beyond the cognitive level and enter into the journey on a personal level.

Since the Spirit of God was sent not only to be studied but ultimately to be experienced, it seems to me we have stopped short of God's intended purpose if we merely discuss and debate His presence instead of exulting in Him on an intimate basis. Long enough have non-charismatic, evangelical Christians (I am both) stood at a distance, frowning and throwing scriptural stones at those in God's family who do not dot every *i* or cross each *t* exactly the same as we. At the same time, long enough has the "lunatic fringe" of a few extremists been allowed to speak for all Christendom, leaving the impression that they are the standard and representative of the majority (they are neither).

What we need is a balanced, experiential view of the Spirit. It should be biblical, of course. Without that we are awash. But it cannot stop at sterile, heady truth on the printed page. It also must be personal, deeply and intimately personal. Without that we miss the whole purpose for which He was sent. In addition, we become defensive in attitude, resistant in spirit, and even arrogant in knowledge—ironically, all the things that grieve the Spirit and keep Him at a distance.

While I can understand the zeal and desire that prompt such things, I am saddened by the outcome: fractured bones and painful bruises in the body of Christ. As our love and respect for one another diminish, the unity we are commanded to keep breaks down and the walls between us get thicker.

Let's face it, most of us are intrigued by the Holy Spirit. Like moths we are attracted to the warmth and the light of His flame. Our desire is to come closer . . . to draw nearer, to know Him more fully and intimately, to enter into new and stimulating dimensions of His workings . . . without getting burned. I know that is true of me, and I suspect you often feel the same.

During my growing-up years, including my years in seminary, I kept a safe distance. I was taught to be careful, to study Him from a doctrinal distance but not to enter into any of the realms of His supernatural workings or to tolerate the possibility of such. Explaining the Spirit was acceptable and encouraged; experiencing Him was neither. Today, I regret that. I have lived long enough and ministered broadly enough to realize that flying closer to the flame is not only possible, it is precisely what God wants.

He is interested in transforming us from the inside out. Flying closer to the flame sets that in motion. He is at work in dozens of different ways, some of them supernatural. Flying closer to the flame makes us acutely aware of that. He is interested in showing us the Father's will and providing us with the dynamics necessary for experiencing satisfaction, joy, peace, and contentment *in spite of our circumstances*. Flying closer to the flame gives us the correct perspective for entering into those (and so many other) experiences. Isn't it time we did?

If you are totally fulfilled in your Christian experience, seldom frustrated, and rarely dissatisfied with yourself, this is not a book for you. Furthermore, if you do not long for a more intimate and uninterrupted relationship with the living God, where you and He are "in sync" and where you regularly sense His presence and power, you don't need to read the pages that follow.

But if you wonder whether you may be missing out on something spiritually . . . or if you desire to move from merely an intellectual faith to an intimate relationship with God . . . or if you would love to explore new regions and realms of His Word that you are intrigued by but have tended to shy away from lest you get burned by "becoming too emotional" or "falling into error," this is the book for you. Fly with me, won't you?

If you are one of the vast number of people who have never known the joy, the sheer ecstasy of walking more intimately with God, yet have known there was more . . . so much more . . . I pray that these pages will draw you in, calm your fears, encourage you to come closer and know the warmth of His eternal flame. I understand what you have been going through . . . and I welcome you as a fellow pilgrim who is weary of a sterile, unproductive, predictable existence. Jesus' promise of an "abundant life" surely includes more than that!

I am absolutely convinced that there are phenomenal and thrilling things hidden in the Scriptures, awaiting discovery and application. I am equally confident that such discoveries and applications will open new vistas of the walk of faith that many have never given themselves permission to view or enjoy. No need to be shy or afraid. As Jesus promised, "the Spirit of truth . . . will guide you into all the truth." As He uses these pages to do just that, we can anticipate unspeakable joy with incredible results.

So come along and journey with me as we, together, fly closer to the flame.

Chuck Swindoll
Fullerton, California
Fall 1993

1

*Let's Get Reacquainted
with the Spirit*

MISS THOMPSON HAD A TOUGH TASK. Her Sunday school lesson plan called for teaching her primary class about the Trinity. It was difficult enough holding their attention with stories and creative object lessons, but when it came to keeping them interested in the identity, attributes, and purpose of the Father, Son, and Spirit . . . well, that was next to impossible.

While thinking through her lesson, she had a creative thought: She would use a big, thick pretzel, with its three holes in the middle. Perfect!

When Sunday morning came she stood before her class, holding the pretzel high in the air, explaining how it was made up of one strand of dough but was so intricately interwoven that there were three distinct holes, each one having its own special shape.

She pointed first to the hole at the top. "Children, this is like God the Father. Think of this first hole as your heavenly Father." She then pointed to the second, explaining slowly and carefully, "This is like God the Son. Think of the hole here on the right as Jesus, your Savior." The class of fresh little faces seemed to be following her with keen interest, so she continued, "And this third hole is God the Holy Ghost. Just as this is one pretzel made up of three separate holes, so the Trinity is one unit made up of three distinct Persons: Father, Son, and Holy Ghost."

Miss Thompson had the children repeat those names aloud: "Father . . . Son . . . and Holy Ghost." Again and again she had the class say the names.

Hoping to cement this concept in their minds, she singled out little Johnny, sitting close to the front, and asked him if he could repeat the names of the "holey" members of the Trinity for the rest of the class. Though reluctant, he slowly stood to his feet and took the pretzel she held out to him.

"This here is God . . . God the Father," he said, pointing to the first hole." (Miss Thompson smiled with delight.) "And this one is Jesus." (Again she beamed over his excellent memory.) "And this third one is . . . uh . . . the *Holy Smoke.*"

Such stories make us smile, often recalling with amusement our own childish "bloopers." But if the truth were told, many adults could not even come that close. To most folks, the person, work, and ministry of the Holy Spirit are a mystery. He is not only invisible but also confusing and even a little bit eerie . . . especially when, for years, He was referred to as "It" and formally addressed as "the Holy *Ghost.*"

All of us have had earthly fathers, so trying to understand the concept of a heavenly Father is not all that difficult. In traditional homes, the father is the one who is in charge, making the big decisions and being ultimately responsible for the family's overall direction, leadership, and stability. There are exceptions and room for discussion, but in the final analysis, it is Dad who casts the final vote.

The Son of God is not difficult to identify either. He was born as a human being and grew up alongside His mother, much like we did. Because He was a flesh-and-blood person, there is little mystery surrounding our mental image of Christ, and His role as the Son of God is fairly clear to us. Our familiarity with His suffering and death causes us to feel close to Him and grateful for Him. He is the One who has implemented the Father's plan.

But the Holy *Ghost?* Not even changing His title to "Spirit" helps that much. Certainly to the uninitiated the name still sounds borderline weird. If His name is vague, it is no surprise that most find His work and ministry the same. And since those who attempt to explain His workings are usually theologians, who are often notoriously deep and unclear themselves, it is no wonder the general public doesn't have a clue to understanding what He is about—to say nothing of feeling intimately related to Him. To many, He is still the divine "It."

Candidly, I am just as culpable as those complex-thinking theologians who have attempted to "explain" the inscrutable Spirit of God. Way back in the 1960s I taught a course on the third member of the Trinity. When I picked up my pen to write this book, I thought it might be helpful to glance over those old notes. My immediate problem was locating them! Had I filed them under *H* for "Holy Spirit"? No. How about *S* for "Spirit"? Nope. Maybe they were tucked away in my subject file under the letter *G* as in "Holy Ghost"? Wrong again. Or *T* for "Trinity"? Not a chance. I stayed at it until I unearthed them . . . filed under *P* for *Pneumatology*. That ought to tell you a lot about how I approached the subject three decades ago: strictly theoretical and theological and not at all relational.

Don't get me wrong. There is nothing—absolutely nothing—wrong with theology. Sound doctrine gives us strong roots. Those who lack such stability can easily fall into extremism and error. However, to track a subject this intimate strictly from an impersonal distance, keeping everything safely theoretical and coolly analytical, won't cut it. There has been too much of that already! What we need is a much more personal investigation of the intimate workings of the Spirit without losing our anchor on theological truth.

Admittedly, some of the Spirit's workings are more theoretical than experiential. For example:

- He is God—co-equal, co-existent, and co-eternal with the Father and the Son.
- He possesses all the attributes of Deity.
- He regenerates the believing sinner.
- He baptizes us into the universal body of Christ.
- He indwells all who have been converted.
- He seals us, keeping every believer securely in the family of God.

And there are a dozen or more equally significant character-istics and workings I could name. These things are all true, but there is *so much more* we've hardly acknowledged, to say nothing of experienced. And though true, they make virtually *no difference* in our conscious existence!

- Why should it thrill anyone to be able to explain the difference between grieving the Spirit and quenching the Spirit? So what if the day-to-day evidences of His power are absent?

- How does it help anyone all that much to know that the Greek term, translated "Helper" or "Comforter" in the New Testament, is *Parakletos*? Does that do anything for us? Are we able to relate to God better because we know that fact?

- Who cares if you and I can define the presence and work of the Holy Spirit prior to and after Pentecost? At the risk of being tarred and feathered, I no longer get excited about such distinctions, especially since many who love to debate those distinctions seem so out of touch with the intimacies of the Spirit's presence on a personal level.

- And what's the big deal about whether He does this or that before, during, or after the Great Tribulation? Those subjects may excite a handful of heady intellectu-als tucked away in the cloistered classrooms of a semi-nary, but, believe me, they mean next to nothing to someone who is running out of hope and needs God's touch desperately.

Get real! We don't need another theological encyclopedia on pneumatology nearly as much as we need an easy-to-understand volume on the practical difference the Spirit can make in our lives on a personal and lasting level. And that's what this book is all about: not "Holy Smoke," but real-to-life reasons we need the

Spirit . . . and the incredible difference He can make in the way we live on a personal basis.

Where Are We Going in This Book?

I have decided to go after the real issues and the practical side of the Holy Spirit—mainly the seldom-mentioned dimensions of His work with us individually and His ministry among us collectively. Why? Because these are the things that give us an edge on living in a sin-cursed world, surrounded by people who have lost their verve for life. It is when these things come alive in us that we become unique instruments in God's hands. I believe that's what you really want, and, I can assure you, I do too!

Let's get specific. Here are some examples of things we are going to be looking into as the succeeding chapters unfold—a random sampling with accompanying Scriptures.

1. The "testifying" work of the Spirit. Have you ever wondered what Paul meant when he told his friends from Ephesus:

> "And now, behold, bound in spirit, I am on my way to Jerusalem, not knowing what will happen to me there, except that the Holy Spirit solemnly testifies to me in every city, saying that bonds and afflictions await me."
> Acts 20:22–23

2. The Spirit's "groanings" as well as His "interceding" on our behalf:

> For we know that the whole creation groans and suffers the pains of childbirth together until now. And not only this, but also we ourselves, having the first fruits of the Spirit, even we ourselves groan within ourselves, waiting eagerly for our adoption as sons, the redemption of our body. . . .
> And in the same way the Spirit also helps our weakness; for we do not know how to pray as we should, but the Spirit Himself intercedes for us with groanings too deep for words;

and He who searches the hearts knows what the mind of the Spirit is, because He intercedes for the saints according to the will of God.

Romans 8:22–23, 26–27

3. Another curious work of the Holy Spirit about which very little has been written has to do with His "searching all things," including "even the depths of God." And what about His revealing those things to us? Talk about intriguing!

But just as it is written,

"THINGS WHICH EYE HAS NOT SEEN AND
    EAR HAS NOT HEARD,
AND WHICH HAVE NOT ENTERED THE
    HEART OF MAN,
ALL THAT GOD HAS PREPARED FOR THOSE
    WHO LOVE HIM."

For to us God revealed them through the Spirit; for the Spirit searches all things, even the depths of God. For who among men knows the thoughts of a man except the spirit of the man, which is in him? Even so the thoughts of God no one knows except the Spirit of God. Now we have received, not the spirit of the world, but the Spirit who is from God, that we might know the things freely given to us by God, which things we also speak, not in words taught by human wisdom, but in those taught by the Spirit, combining spiritual thoughts with spiritual words.

1 Corinthians 2:9–13

All my adult life I have heard about, as well as affirmed, the ministry of the *Word*. I still believe in it—now more than ever. But there is more. There is also the ministry of *God!* As His Spirit probes the Father's "depths" and searches those mysterious, unfathomable labyrinths of His will and His truth, He teaches them to us by "combining spiritual thoughts with spiritual words." We shall dig deeply into what that means.

4. Another "unmentionable" would be the "anointing" of

the Spirit, referred to in earlier versions of the English Bible as the "unction" of the Spirit.

> Children, it is the last hour; and just as you heard that antichrist is coming, even now many antichrists have arisen; from this we know that it is the last hour. They went out from us, but they were not really of us; for if they had been of us, they would have remained with us; but they went out, in order that it might be shown that they all are not of us. But you have an anointing from the Holy One, and you all know.
>
> 1 John 2:18–20

5. Periodically, someone will suggest that we should "test the spirits." In some unusual manner such "testing" helps us "know the Spirit of God," according to the apostle John. Perhaps you have wondered about these words for years, as I have:

> Beloved, do not believe every spirit, but test the spirits to see whether they are from God; because many false prophets have gone out into the world. By this you know the Spirit of God: every spirit that confesses that Jesus Christ has come in the flesh is from God; and every spirit that does not confess Jesus is not from God; and this is the spirit of the antichrist, of which you have heard that it is coming, and now it is already in the world.
>
> 1 John 4:1–3

6. John also writes about the "witness" of the Spirit, another curious comment very few ever bother to examine.

> And who is the one who overcomes the world, but he who believes that Jesus is the Son of God? This is the one who came by water and blood, Jesus Christ; not with the water only, but with the water and with the blood. And it is the Spirit who bears witness, because the Spirit is the truth. For there are three that bear witness, the Spirit and the water and the blood; and the three are in agreement. If we receive the witness of men, the witness of God is greater; for the

witness of God is this, that He has borne witness concerning His Son.

1 John 5:5–9

I think you're getting the drift of where we are going. In the process, I want to address certain terms that have been linked with the Spirit of God: terms like *power* and *presence, revelation* and *visions, miracles* and *healings,* even *intuition, guidance,* and *God's voice.* How seldom we feel comfortable addressing these subjects, but we need to have a better understanding of them if we hope to fly closer to the flame.

Even though we are not one full chapter into the book, some of you are probably getting uneasy . . . almost as if you feel guilty or afraid. Perhaps you're starting to wonder about me. *Maybe Chuck's getting a little weird with all that wind blowing on him on the Harley . . . and from hanging around those strange-looking motorcycle riders. Yep, that must be it!*

Wrong.

I've been turning these things over in my mind for more than two decades. In fact, I can remember sitting in a seminary classroom wondering why certain verses weren't mentioned or why the professor seemed uptight and defensive when some young man pressed him a little strongly on verses he had chosen to bypass.

Or perhaps you are feeling a little nervous about the direction I might take on some of these controversial issues.

Relax! We have everything to gain and nothing to lose by allowing the truth to emerge. It's the truth, remember, that sets us free. So let's not rush to judgment or try to find some popular label or theological category in which to dump these things. Nor should we ever be afraid of the flame!

The inescapable fact is this: Most (yes, most) Christians you and I know have very little dynamic or joy in their lives. Just ask them. They long for depth, for passion, for a satisfying peace and stability instead of a superficial relationship with God made up of words without feelings and struggles without healings. Surely there is more to the life of faith than church meetings, Bible study, religious jargon, and periodic prayers. Surely the awesome Spirit of God wishes to do more within us than what is presently going on! There are scars He wants to remove. There are fractured feelings He wants to heal. There are insights He longs to reveal. There are profound dimensions of life He would dearly love to open up. But none of the above will happen automatically—not as long as He remains a sterile, untouchable blip on our theological PC.

He is the comforting Helper, remember? He is the Truth-Teacher, the will-of-the-Father Revealer, the Gift-Giver, the Hurt-Healer. He is the inextinguishable flame of God, my friend. *HE IS GOD.* To remain at a distance from Him is worse than wrong; it is downright *tragic.* Flying closer to the flame, therefore, is better than good; it is absolutely *magnificent.*

Discovering the Spirit's Significance

Maybe all this emphasis on the Holy Spirit seems overdrawn to you. Could it be that you have never been shown from the Scriptures just how significant a role the Lord intended Him to play in your life? Before bringing this chapter to a close, let me help you see three contributions He makes, without which life is reduced to dull and gray.

First, His Permanent Presence Within Us

Jesus sat alone with His twelve disciples in a small, second-story room the night before He was crucified. They had a meal together, followed by the Last Supper. Judas was dismissed. Earlier, Jesus had washed His disciples' feet. A brief discussion about that arose. Then, almost without interruption, He "delivered His soul." By that I mean He communicated the most intimate and the most important information and instruction they could hear. His words are found in chapters 14–16 of the Gospel by John, a section that has come to be known as "The Upper Room Discourse." He began:

"Let not your heart be troubled; believe in God, believe also in Me. In My Father's house are many dwelling places; if it were not so, I would have told you; for I go to prepare a place for you. And if I go and prepare a place for you, I will come again, and receive you to Myself; that where I am, there you may be also. And you know the way where I am going." Thomas said to Him, "Lord, we do not know where You are going, how do we know the way?" Jesus said to him, "I am the way, and the truth, and the life; no one comes to the Father, but through Me. . . . I will not leave you as orphans; I will come to you."

John 14:1–6, 18

We sit calmly as we read those words and as we try to imagine the disciples hearing them. But they were *anything* but calm! Jesus was announcing His departure, and they were struggling with feelings of abandonment. Their stomachs must have churned when He used the word "orphans," for that is *exactly* how they felt. For more than three years they had been inseparable. He was there when they awoke. He was with them through virtually every situation they faced. When they called for help, He was usually nearby and able to step in. When they said "Good night," He was there to respond. Suddenly, all that would change. He was leaving them—permanently. And though they were adults, the sting of His departure left them feeling orphaned.

I recall having that feeling when my dad died back in 1980. My mother had passed on nine years earlier; now I was without both parents. I was more than forty-five years old, had a family of my own, and was neck deep in ministry. Nevertheless, his departure marked a passage in my life after which things would never be quite the same. No more visits. No more phone calls. No opportunity to sit and talk through something I was facing . . . to have him listen and respond. In a strange way I felt orphaned, and to this day I still have occasions when I miss being able to see my father, to hear his voice, to watch him respond.

That was how the disciples felt. No more meals together. No more discussions beside the sea. No more quiet talks around the fire at night. No more shared laughter . . . or tears . . . or watching Him handle some thorny situation. Orphaned.

And yet He promised not to leave them as orphans. "Plan B" was already in motion.

> "And I will ask the Father, and He will give you another Helper, that He may be with you forever; that is the Spirit of truth, whom the world cannot receive, because it does not behold Him or know Him, but you know Him because He abides with you, and will be in you."
>
> John 14:16–17

Aha! Jesus promised them that His replacement would be "another Helper," namely, the Holy Spirit. And, unlike Jesus, who had only been with them, He (the Spirit) would be *in* them. Quite a difference! Not too many days hence, when the Spirit would arrive, He would slip inside them and live within them forever. No more temporary companionship; the Spirit's presence would be (and still is) a permanent presence. It had never been like that before. Not even in the lives of those Old Testament greats. But from now on . . . yes!

Jesus' departure was essential in order for the Spirit to begin His permanent indwelling. Jesus said so.

> "But I tell you the truth, it is to your advantage that I go away; for if I do not go away, the Helper shall not come to you; but if I go, I will send Him to you."
>
> John 16:7

So then, we need to turn next to the place in Scripture where Jesus' departure is recorded—Acts 1—to see what He said about the Spirit's coming, for it is there we find the next significant contribution of the Spirit.

Second, His Unparalleled Dynamic Among Us

> And gathering them together, He commanded them not to leave Jerusalem, but to wait for what the Father had prom-

ised, "Which," He said, "you heard of from Me; for John baptized with water, but you shall be baptized with the Holy Spirit not many days from now."

And so when they had come together, they were asking Him, saying, "Lord, is it at this time You are restoring the kingdom to Israel?" He said to them, "It is not for you to know times or epochs which the Father has fixed by His own authority; but you shall receive power when the Holy Spirit has come upon you; and you shall be My witnesses both in Jerusalem, and in all Judea and Samaria, and even to the remotest part of the earth."

Acts 1:4–8

Our Lord's ascension was only moments away. Naturally, He wanted to bid farewell to His closest companions. As they stood alongside, He reassured them: "you shall receive power when the Holy Spirit has come upon you" (v. 8). Not *if* the Spirit comes, but *when*. And upon His arrival, *power* would be received.

Now, Jesus was not saying that power would begin to exist at that point, for power had always been one of God's characteristics. Power was present at Creation. Power opened the Red Sea. Power brought water from the rock and fire from heaven. In fact, it was that same magnificent power that had brought Christ back from beyond at His resurrection. But those kinds of supernatural manifestations were not what He was promising. The disciples would not be creating worlds or parting seas or taking the place of God.

What Christ promised them was enabling power. Another kind of power, as A. T. Robertson correctly observed:

> Not the "power" about which they were concerned (political organization and equipment for the empire on the order of Rome) . . . this new "power" (*dunamin*), to enable them (from *dunamai,* to be able), to grapple with the spread of the gospel in the world.[1]

Jesus was saying, in effect, "You will receive a new enablement, a new dynamic, altogether different from what you have ever experienced before." I would suggest that this promised "power" also included an inner confidence, almost to the point of invincibility, regardless of the odds they were sure to face.

F. F. Bruce, in his splendid volume on the Book of Acts, states that:

> they would be clothed with heavenly power—that power by which, in the event, their mighty works were accomplished and their preaching made effective. As Jesus Himself had been anointed at His baptism with the Holy Spirit and power, so His followers were now to be similarly anointed and enabled to carry on His work.[2]

The power (I prefer to use the term *dynamic*) that Jesus promised the disciples, directly—and us indirectly—was the Spirit's unparalleled help and enablement, which would immeasurably surpass their own human ability.

Think of it! It's the very same dynamic that is resident within every Christian today. But where has it gone? Why is it so seldom evident among us? What can be done to get it in motion as it once was? Those are some of the questions that prompted me to dig deeply into this study.

Third, His Affirming Will for Us

In His statement prior to His departure, Jesus included an additional promise to His disciples. "You shall be My witnesses," He said. The Spirit would free their lips so that they would *witness* consistently of Him. First, in Jerusalem, where they would be located when the Spirit came. Next, in Judea and Samaria, the surrounding regions beyond the city. Ultimately, "even to the remotest part of the earth." The Spirit's presence would spur them on, enabling them to speak openly and boldly of their Savior. He is still longing to do that within and through us today, affirming God's will for us.

A quick glance at the fourth chapter of Acts reveals the results of this Spirit-filled dynamic: *perseverance*. Peter and John had been preaching in the streets of Jerusalem, where they were later arrested, confronted, and threatened by the officials. Undaunted by the threats, the disciples stood toe-to-toe with the officials. Their calm perseverance did not go unnoticed.

> Now as they observed the confidence of Peter and John, and understood that they were uneducated and untrained men, they were marveling, and began to recognize them as having been with Jesus.
>
> Acts 4:13

Why? Why would the religious officials marvel at untrained and unlearned men? Because they were impressed by their firm resolve. Their thoughts might have been: *These are a different kind of men. They are not like the soldiers we deal with or the politicians or our fellow officials.* As a result, they began to recognize that these were Jesus people . . . these were men who had once been with Jesus. How would they know that? *The dynamic!*

Not long afterward, the disciples were called back before the Jewish Supreme Court and told in no uncertain terms to knock it off!

> "We gave you strict orders not to continue teaching in this name, and behold, you have filled Jerusalem with your teaching, and intend to bring this man's blood upon us." But Peter and the apostles answered and said, "We must obey God rather than men."
>
> Acts 5:28–29

Friend, that is persistent, invincible dynamic! Normally folks are intimidated in the official setting of a courtroom. Not those men!

Remember Acts 1:8? "You shall receive power." You'll be witnesses. You'll have perseverance to stand firm, regardless.

A few moments later these same Spirit-enabled men set the record straight:

"The God of our fathers raised up Jesus, whom you had put to death by hanging Him on a cross. He is the one whom God exalted to His right hand as a Prince and a Savior, to grant repentance to Israel, and forgiveness of sins. And we are witnesses of these things; and so is the Holy Spirit, whom God has given to those who obey Him."

Acts 5:30–32

And what happened? Did they lick their wounds and curl up in some cave until the situation cooled down? Were they frightened and disillusioned? On the contrary. Even after they were threatened and brutally beaten,

> . . . they went on their way from the presence of the Council, rejoicing that they had been considered worthy to suffer shame for His name. And every day, in the temple and from house to house, they kept right on teaching and preaching Jesus as the Christ.

Acts 5:41–42

The Spirit's enablement . . . that's heaven-sent "power"! And the good news is that the same Spirit who filled believers in the first century can fill us in the twentieth. And the same dynamic can be ours . . . the same boldness and determination, invincibility and perseverance in the midst of danger.

Removing the Resistance Between Us and Him

Doesn't all of this sound appealing? Haven't you longed for such fortitude, such confident faith? These traits were never meant to be restricted to century-one saints. Nowhere in the Scriptures do I find a statement that limits the Spirit's presence or dynamic to some bygone era. The same One who promised a handful of frightened followers new dimensions of divine enablement is anxious to fulfill that in us today.

Frankly, I'm ready for it, aren't you? We need it, and it is ours to claim . . . so *let's claim it!*

To do so, at least three forces of resistance must be removed. Until we remove them, our hope for that first-century kind of life-changing, supernatural power will remain just that—a hope, a theoretical dream, something we can read about in ancient history but never know firsthand. And what are these forces of resistance?

1. The barrier of the fearful unknown.
2. The wall of traditional limitations.
3. The obstacle course of personal excuses.

Read that list again, only this time pause after each one and think about the presence of that particular resistance in your own life.

I want to close this first chapter with a brief but honest confession: I am not, by nature, a person who changes easily. I was raised by a very stable, consistent mother and father who provided a solid home where my brother, sister, and I grew up securely. We were taught to love God, believe in Christ, trust and obey the Bible, and be faithful in church attendance. Much of my theology was hammered out on the anvil of those early years at home.

As I grew up, my roots were strengthened in the fundamentals of the Christian faith. My training in seminary drove those roots even deeper. By the time I graduated, I had many convictions and few questions, especially in the realm of the Holy Spirit. But during thirty-plus years of ministry both in the United States and abroad, I have come to realize that there are dimensions of the Spirit's ministry I have never tapped. There is also a dynamic power in His presence I have witnessed that I long to know more of firsthand. I now have questions and a strong interest in many of the things of the Spirit I once felt were settled.

I do not fear digging into these intimate and mysterious realms, for He is "the Spirit of truth" and Jesus, my Lord, promised that He would "guide you [us] into all the truth" (John 16:13). I invite you to come with me on this exciting and creative journey. I encourage you not to be afraid as we, together, fly closer to the flame.

As we get reacquainted with the One who lives within us, who knows? We may make some discoveries that will necessitate our shifting here and there in our longstanding theology. No problem. I've seen enough people who have stopped thinking and changing to know that that's not for me. I have the feeling it's not for you either . . . otherwise, you would have already laid this book aside before finishing this first chapter.

If you are still willing to risk, read on. The next chapter moves even closer to the flame.

2

The Main Agenda of God's Spirit: Transformation

*I*N 1983 JOHN SCULLEY QUIT his post at Pepsico to become the president of Apple Computer. He took a big risk leaving his prestigious position with a well-established firm to join ranks with an unproven little outfit that offered no guarantees, only the excitement of one man's transforming vision. Sculley says he made the risky move after Apple cofounder Steve Jobs goaded him with the question, "Do you want to spend the rest of your life selling sugared water or do you want a chance to change the world?"

The original disciples were a handful of unlikely misfits, nothing more than a "rather ragged aggregation of souls," as Robert Coleman puts it in his *Master Plan of Evangelism*.[1] But the remarkable fact is that they were the same ones who later "turned the world upside down," according to the testimony of people in the first century. How can anyone explain the transformation? Was it some crash course they took, some upbeat seminar on leadership? No. Then maybe it was really the work of angels, but the disciples were given credit for it? No, the biblical record clearly states that it was the same group of once-timid men Jesus had trained. Perhaps some high-powered "heavenly drug," some miracle-inducing chemical, was inserted into their bodies that changed the men overnight? *Enough!*

There is only one intelligent answer: It was the arrival and the empowerment of the Holy Spirit. He alone transformed those frightened, awkward, reluctant men into strong-hearted, unintimidated, invincible prophets of God. Instead of feeling abandoned and orphaned, instead of spending the rest of their lives with "sugared water," they became directly involved in changing the world. Once the Spirit took up residence with them, once He was given complete control of their lives, He put His agenda into full operation, and they were never the same. They embodied His dynamic. They no longer held back or stood in the shadows or looked for excuses not to be engaged in obeying their Lord's mandate to "go and make disciples of all nations." Once "another Helper" came, transformation occurred . . . immediate transformation.

A Brief Glance at the "Orphaned" Disciples

To appreciate this transformation as fully as we should, we need a before-and-after portrait of the men who walked with Christ. Let's start with the scene we glanced at earlier in chapter 1—the Last Supper.

Judas had left. The meal had been eaten. The taste of bread and wine were still on their tongues as their Lord began to unveil the reality of His departure. Their stomachs churned with the thought of going on without Him. They were troubled, even though He urged them, "Let not your heart be troubled . . ." (John 14:1). They were confused, as Thomas's question reveals, "Lord, we do not know where You are going, how do we know the way?" (John 14:5). Another in the group was bothered about the change in plans as he asked, "Lord, what then has happened that You are going to disclose Yourself to us, and not to the world?" (John 14:22).

Later, Peter denied Him . . . and He was the leader of the group (Mark 14:53–72)! Ultimately, when push came to shove, "all the disciples left Him and fled" (Matt. 26:56). Every last one of them deserted their Master.

At His resurrection they were surprised at the thought of His body not being in the tomb. And that same evening, after knowing of His resurrection, the disciples were hiding out together behind closed doors. Why? They were hiding "for fear of the

Jews" (John 20:19). If that were not enough, even after He came among some of them, Thomas firmly resisted, declaring he had to witness everything firsthand or (in his own words) "I will not believe" (John 20:25).

Troubled, confused, bothered, disloyal, fearful, doubting . . . these men were anything but valiant warriors for Christ. Prior to the Spirit's transforming work, they were wimps! To them, when the original game plan was aborted, the mission was considered *unaccomplished.*

I often return to Coleman's realistic description of the disciples. It is anything but flattering.

> What is more revealing about these men is that at first they do not impress us as being key men. None of them occupied prominent places in the Synagogue, nor did any of them belong to the Levitical priesthood. For the most part they were common laboring men, probably having no professional training beyond the rudiments of knowledge necessary for their vocation. Perhaps a few of them came from families of some considerable means, such as the sons of Zebedee, but none of them could have been considered wealthy. They had no academic degrees in the arts and philosophies of their day. Like their Master, their formal education likely consisted only of the Synagogue schools. Most of them were raised in the poor section of the country around Galilee. Apparently the only one of the twelve who came from the more refined region of Judea was Judas Iscariot. By any standard of sophisticated culture then and now they would surely be considered as a rather ragged aggregation of souls. One might wonder how Jesus could ever use them. They were impulsive, temperamental, easily offended, and had all the prejudices of their environment. In short, these men selected by the Lord to be His assistants represented an average cross section of the lot of society in their day. Not the kind of group one would expect to win the world for Christ.[2]

You may not appreciate such a forthright portrayal of the disciples, but from what I read of them in the Gospel accounts, it is accurate. Prior to the coming of the Spirit and His transforming presence in their lives, they bore all the marks of men least likely to survive, to say nothing of succeed.

An Enlightening Discovery of Personal Transformation

Jesus knew His men much better than they knew themselves. He knew Judas was deceptive and Peter was rash. He knew Thomas struggled with doubt and that John was a dreamer. He knew how petty and competitive they were . . . how selfish and fragile. He knew the final Eleven thought of themselves as fiercely loyal, but when the chips were down, they would slink into the shadows. He knew that a new dynamic was imperative if His mission for the establishment of the church and the evangelization of the world had any hope of being accomplished. Therefore, when He promised "another Helper," He meant One who would transform them from the inside out. He knew that the only way they would ultimately do "greater works" than He had accomplished would be through the Spirit's presence and power.

Little did the disciples realize how much they lacked. Most of them (perhaps all of them) thought they had more going for them than was the case. Peter, remember, assured his Lord, "I will lay down my life for You," and "Even though all may fall away, yet I will not" (John 13:37; Mark 14:29). What a comedown when they later realized that they were not nearly as resilient or loyal or courageous as they had assured Him they would be.

We've all been there, haven't we? About the time we get out on a limb thinking we're pretty capable, we get sawed off by a sudden and embarrassing discovery. At that point we realize we aren't nearly as effective or competent as we had convinced ourselves we were.

I read a classic example of this recently in Max DePree's splendid volume, *Leadership Jazz.*

> The story goes that a German machine tool company once developed a very fine bit for drilling holes in steel. The tiny bit

could bore a hole about the size of a human hair. This seemed like a tremendously valuable innovation. The Germans sent samples off to Russia, the United States, and Japan, suggesting that this bit was the ultimate in machining technology.

From the Russians, they heard nothing. From the Americans came a quick response inquiring as to the price of the bits, available discounts, and the possibility of a licensing arrangement.

After some delay, there was the predictable, polite response from the Japanese, complimenting the Germans on their achievement, but with a postscript noting that the Germans' bit was enclosed with a slight alteration. Excitedly, the German engineers opened the package, carefully examined their bit, and to their amazement discovered that the Japanese had bored a neat hole through it.[3]

When the Spirit of God bored His way into the lives of those awaiting His arrival in that upstairs room somewhere in Jerusalem, His transforming presence was immediately evident. As I read what transpired in the early part of the Book of Acts, I am able to identify at least four transforming changes among those who received the Spirit.

First, *their human frailties were transformed into supernatural gifts and abilities.*

From the moment the Holy Spirit arrived, nothing about the disciples remained the same. When His power, His dynamic (the Greek term is *dunamis*) fell upon them, they even spoke in another language.

> And when the day of Pentecost had come, they were all together in one place. And suddenly there came from heaven a noise like a violent, rushing wind, and it filled the whole house where they were sitting. And there appeared to them tongues as of fire distributing themselves, and they rested on each one of them. And they were all filled with the Holy Spirit and began to speak with other tongues, as the Spirit was giving them utterance.
>
> Acts 2:1–4

Try to imagine those phenomena occurring back to back.

- A noise, an incredibly loud roar (the Greek term is the word from which we get our English word *echo*), not unlike the sound of a violent hurricane unleashing its earsplitting fury on some coastal village.
- A large "ball" of fire, spontaneously separating into smaller flames, each in the shape of a tongue that came to rest upon each person in the room.
- As this occurred, each of the individuals was simultaneously "filled with the Holy Spirit." From their lips flowed words they had never spoken before in languages they had never learned.

This experience completely revolutionized their lives. Those who had been troubled and fearful no longer struggled with those feelings. The once frightened, unsure, confused, timid men never again evidenced such inadequacies. From that time on they were bold in faith and confident in their God. They were *transformed*.

Suddenly they were able to speak in languages not their own. So clear and accurate were those languages that those who heard them were shocked.

And when this sound occurred, the multitude came together, and were bewildered, because they were each one hearing them speak in his own language. And they were amazed and marveled, saying, "Why, are not all these who are speaking Galileans? And how is it that we each hear them in our own language to which we were born? Parthians and Medes and Elamites, and residents of Mesopotamia, Judea and Cappadocia, Pontus and Asia, Phrygia and Pamphylia, Egypt and the districts of Libya around Cyrene, and visitors from Rome, both Jews and proselytes, Cretans and Arabs—we hear them in our own tongues speaking of the mighty deeds of God."

Acts 2:6–11

It is noteworthy that the original term used for "language" in verses 6 and 8 is the Greek word *dialektos,* from which we get "dialect." Remarkable! Those untrained, monolingual Galileans were suddenly able to communicate in the native dialects of individuals from regions far removed from Palestine.

And if that were not enough, some in the group were given the supernatural ability to touch another life and restore physical health.

> Now Peter and John were going up to the temple at the ninth hour, the hour of prayer. And a certain man who had been lame from his mother's womb was being carried along, whom they used to set down every day at the gate of the temple which is called Beautiful, in order to beg alms of those who were entering the temple. And when he saw Peter and John about to go into the temple, he began asking to receive alms. And Peter, along with John, fixed his gaze upon him and said, "Look at us!" And he began to give them his attention, expecting to receive something from them. But Peter said, "I do not possess silver and gold, but what I do have I give to you: In the name of Jesus Christ the Nazarene—walk!" And seizing him by the right hand, he raised him up; and immediately his feet and his ankles were strengthened. And with a leap, he stood upright and began to walk; and he entered the temple with them, walking and leaping and praising God.
>
> Acts 3:1–8

Before we get the idea that these men suddenly "glowed" with some kind of aura or in some other way appeared different, however, let's hear the testimony of Peter:

> And while he was clinging to Peter and John, all the people ran together to them at the so-called portico of Solomon, full of amazement. But when Peter saw this, he replied to the people, "Men of Israel, why do you marvel at this, or why do you gaze at us, as if by our own power or piety we had made him walk?"
>
> Acts 3:11–12

Clearly, Peter and John were still "just plain Peter and John." They didn't promote themselves as miracle workers or divine healers. They seemed to be as amazed over this as those who witnessed what had happened. Having been transformed by the Helper whom Jesus had sent, the disciples did not turn the scene into a man-glorifying sideshow.

Second, *their fearful reluctance was transformed into bold confidence.*

Remember an earlier scene when these same men, afraid of being found out by the Jews, hid silently behind closed doors? The last thing they wanted was to be pointed out as followers of Jesus. They were frozen in fear.

No longer. According to this narrative, they poured into the public streets of Jerusalem preaching Christ and urging total strangers to repent and to believe in the name of Jesus.

> And with many other words he [Peter] solemnly testified and kept on exhorting them, saying, "Be saved from this perverse generation!"
>
> Acts 2:40

Later, when Peter and John had been arrested and were being interrogated, their quiet confidence did not go unnoticed:

> Now as they observed the confidence of Peter and John, and understood that they were uneducated and untrained men, they were marveling, and began to recognize them as having been with Jesus.
>
> Acts 4:13

The followers of Jesus didn't look any different physically. They didn't suddenly become learned men. Nor were they abruptly made cultured and sophisticated. No, they remained rawboned fishermen and a couple of "good ol' boys." But deep within their beings, down inside, they were nothing like they had been. They were *transformed.*

Third, *their fears and intimidation were transformed into a sense of invincibility.*

Webster states that intimidation is timidity, being afraid, overawed, deterred with threats. These men, having been invaded by God's Spirit, were none of the above.

- Instead of running from the public, they ran toward them.
- Instead of hoping not to be seen, they exhorted total strangers to repent.
- Instead of being frightened by insults, warnings, and threats, they stood face-to-face with their accusers and did not blink. When told to keep it quiet, they answered unflinchingly, "We must obey God rather than men" (Acts 5:29).

Even when called before the Council, the supreme ruling body of the Jews, this handful of "uneducated and untrained men" stood like steers in a blizzard. They weren't about to back down, even if they were forced to stand before some of the same prejudiced and cruel judges who had unjustly manipulated the trials against Jesus of Nazareth. They refused to be overawed. Such invincible courage!

Where does one get such boldness today? From studying at Oxford or Yale or Harvard? Hardly. How about from reading the biographies of great men and women? That may stimulate our minds, but it cannot transform our lives. Then perhaps the secret of such boldness is a mentor, someone whose walk with God is admirable and consistent. Again, as helpful as heroes and models may be, their influence cannot suddenly infuse us with invincible courage. The Spirit of God alone is able to make that happen.

It was not until He came and filled those frail and frightened men with His supernatural "dynamic" that they were genuinely (and permanently) changed deep within—*transformed*.

Fourth, *their lonely, grim feelings of abandonment were transformed into joyful perseverance.*

On the heels of their second arrest, Peter and John let out all the stops! Refusing to tell their frowning accusers what they wanted to hear, they looked them squarely in the eye and pulled no punches.

> And when they had brought them, they stood them before the Council. And the high priest questioned them, saying, "We gave you strict orders not to continue teaching in this name, and behold, you have filled Jerusalem with your teaching, and intend to bring this man's blood upon us." But Peter and the apostles answered and said, "We must obey God rather than men. The God of our fathers raised up Jesus, whom you had put to death by hanging Him on a cross. He is the one whom God exalted to His right hand as a Prince and a Savior, to grant repentance to Israel, and forgiveness of sins. And we are witnesses of these things; and so is the Holy Spirit, whom God has given to those who obey Him."
>
> Acts 5:27–32

I find it absolutely amazing that those men, once so petty and competitive and self-centered, are now so strong-hearted, so incredibly confident. So did the officials.

> But when they heard this, they were cut to the quick and were intending to slay them. But a certain Pharisee named Gamaliel, a teacher of the Law, respected by all the people, stood up in the Council and gave orders to put the men outside for a short time. And he said to them, "Men of Israel, take care what you propose to do with these men. For sometime ago Theudas rose up, claiming to be somebody; and a group of about four hundred men joined up with him. And he was slain; and all who followed him were dispersed and came to nothing. After this man Judas of Galilee rose up in the days of the census, and drew away some people after him, he too perished, and all those who followed him were scattered. And so in the present case, I say to you, stay away from these men and let them alone, for if this plan or action should be of men, it will be overthrown; but if it is of God, you will not be able to overthrow them; or else you may even be found fighting against God." And they took his advice;

and after calling the apostles in, they flogged them and ordered them to speak no more in the name of Jesus, and then released them.

Acts 5:33–40

The Jewish leaders must have thought, "That ought to do it. A firm warning, a bloody flogging, and this strong threat ought to shut them up for good!"

It didn't. As we saw earlier,

So they went on their way from the presence of the Council, rejoicing that they had been considered worthy to suffer shame for His name. And every day, in the temple and from house to house, they kept right on teaching and preaching Jesus as the Christ.

Acts 5:41–42

The Amplified Bible says they were "dignified by the indignity."

The flogging, the warning, and the threat merely fueled the fire of their determination. In fact (did you catch it?), they left "rejoicing." And upon their return to the company of their friends, joy filled everyone's hearts, not sadness . . . not disillusionment. The wimps had become warriors!

The Spirit of God may have reminded them of the words of their now-departed Lord: "In the world you have tribulation, but take courage; I have overcome the world" (John 16:33). In fact, Peter himself would later write:

Beloved, do not be surprised at the fiery ordeal among you, which comes upon you for your testing, as though some strange thing were happening to you; but to the degree that you share the sufferings of Christ, keep on rejoicing; so that also at the revelation of His glory, you may rejoice with exultation.

1 Peter 4:12–13

Quite likely he was recalling that day when he and John had been dragged before the Council and unfairly beaten. Instead of wondering, "Why did the Lord leave us alone?" or "Where is He when we need Him?" their joyful perseverance won the day. No resentment. No feelings of abandonment. No pity party for PLOM members only (Poor Little Ol' Me).

Why? Because the disciples had been radically changed. Not merely motivated or momentarily mesmerized—they were *transformed*.

A Straightforward Analysis of How It Happened

But how? What did it? How could these same men who had earlier run for cover now stand tall, refusing to be backed down or even whipped down?

One possible explanation that comes to mind is *positive thinking*. Maybe one or two in the little band of disciples looked around and said, "Now that Christ has left, it is time for us to look at the bright side of things and be responsible."

Very, very doubtful. Positive thinking doesn't go very far when folks are getting the skin beaten off their backs—and it certainly doesn't keep them rejoicing in the midst of it. Nor does positive thinking suddenly change a person who is naturally and normally intimidated into one who is invincible. Having a positive attitude is a wonderful thing, but it is unable to bring about wholesale transformation.

Another possibility is a *better environment*. Maybe things lightened up. Perhaps the public had a change of heart and became more open and willing to accept responsibility for crucifying Christ. Caesar himself may have decided that followers of Christ were not really that much of a concern to the mighty Roman Empire.

You're smiling. You know that things got increasingly more hostile, more intense.

Well, perhaps someone *taught a seminar* on "How to Endure Suffering: Twelve Steps Toward a Successful Life."

No, you know better.

If you ever go to Rome, spend some time in the catacombs. Walk slowly through the narrow, labyrinthine paths that lead deep into the bowels of that subterranean world and you will see sights you'll never forget. You will feel like groaning as you stare at slender little berths where broken bodies were placed. You may even see the writings or touch the sign of the fish or a cross, a crown, or some other equally eloquent, albeit mute, reminder of pain. As you brush along those ancient graves in silence, much of the superficial stuff you read today about being happy through suffering will seem terribly shallow. At the same time, the few signs that pulsate with true triumph in Christ will take on new meaning. What you will witness firsthand will be the evidence of transformed lives.

The Best (and Only) Conclusion

No course was taught. No cheerleader led the disciples in mind-bending chants that gave them a positive attitude. No change in environment brought about their transformation. It was the Spirit of God and nothing else. It was the life-changing, attitude-altering, dynamic power of the living Lord that swept over them and became permanently resident within them.

Remember Jesus' promises? Let me quickly review several of them:

> "Truly, truly, I say to you, he who believes in Me, the works that I do shall he do also; and greater works than these shall he do; because I go to the Father."
>
> John 14:12

> "And I will ask the Father, and He will give you another Helper, that He may be with you forever; that is the Spirit of truth, whom the world cannot receive, because it does not behold Him or know Him, but you know Him because He abides with you, and will be in you. I will not leave you as orphans; I will come to you."
>
> John 14:16–18

"But the Helper, the Holy Spirit, whom the Father will send in My name, He will teach you all things, and bring to your remembrance all that I said to you."

John 14:26

"But you shall receive power when the Holy Spirit has come upon you; and you shall be My witnesses both in Jerusalem, and in all Judea and Samaria, and even to the remotest part of the earth."

Acts 1:8

God kept His word. And the disciples were never the same.

A Probing Question Only You Can Answer

Is the Spirit of God being allowed to transform *your* life? In case you think that's an irrelevant question, read the opening words of Romans 12:

I urge you therefore, brethren, by the mercies of God, to present your bodies a living and holy sacrifice, acceptable to God, which is your spiritual service of worship. And do not be conformed to this world, but be transformed by the renewing of your mind, that you may prove what the will of God is, that which is good and acceptable and perfect.

Romans 12:1–2

Don't miss the twofold command: "Do not be *conformed* . . . but be *transformed*" (italics mine).

Are you honest enough with yourself to answer my question? Is the Holy Spirit being allowed to transform your life?

There are only two possible answers: yes or no. If your answer is no, there are two possible reasons. Either you do not have the Spirit within you (i.e., you're not a Christian), or He is there but you prefer to live life on your own. I'll address that in more detail in the pages that follow. For now . . . let me urge you to do some soul-searching.

Speaking in tongues or healing the lame or explaining the supernatural phenomena recorded in the early section of the Book of Acts are intriguing subjects and, of course, important. But they can so easily become theological smoke screens, points of debate, and safe places in which to hide from the hard, probing question regarding you and your personal life.

My main concern is the Spirit's main agenda: Are *you* allowing *Him* to transform *your life?* If not, why not?

Flying closer to the flame may seem risky . . . but it is the best place to be. In fact, it is the only way to live.

3

My Sin . . . and "The Things of the Spirit"

I WAS MINISTERING AT A CONFERENCE with my long-time musical colleague, Dr. Howard Stevenson. He was leading the conferees in the singing of several wonderful choruses of worship, as only Howie can do it, and decided to teach everyone some very meaningful and tender motions to the old chorus "Spirit of the Living God." One of the motions involved our holding our hands up as we sang "Fill me . . . use me." It was handled so tastefully and graciously by Howie that I was confident everyone would participate. Wrong. Later, a few mentioned that they didn't know Howie and I were "charismatics" (the way they said it, the label sounded almost like a term of profanity).

What a ridiculous, rigid, and narrow response! Since when is there anything wrong with lifting our hands to God in praise and worship? It is biblical, you know. And since when does a certain posture deserve a label? It wasn't uncommon for folks in biblical days to fall prostrate before God in humiliation and prayer. Wonder what we would be called if we started doing that?

We need to take God out of our man-made box.

To make that happen, we need to relax a little. No, relax *a lot!* We need to be less defensive, less intense, and allow the truth of God to speak for itself. If that means changing here or there, so be it. Never forget, it is truth that sets us free. If you are missing out on all He wants to do in you and through you, then, in the words of the late British writer J. B. Phillips, your God is too small.[1]

Yet, at the same time, we must treat Him with the awesome honor He deserves. Flying closer to the flame does not suggest a disrespectful or casual familiarity with a holy God, but rather a more spontaneous, intimate, and dynamic relationship with Him who delights in our calling Him "Abba, Father." The key to such intimacy is the Holy Spirit. For too long we have kept our distance instead of pulling up closer and giving ourselves permission to worship and walk with Him in fresh and creative ways.

We need to maintain a healthy balance between being careful and being open. Being careful should not make us resistant to truth any more than being open should lead us into error.

Martin Lloyd-Jones, that superb expositor who served London's Westminster Chapel for more than twenty years, expressed it well:

> We must be very careful in these matters. What do we know of the realm of the Spirit? What do we know of the Spirit falling on people? What do we know about these great manifestations of the Holy Spirit? We need to be very careful "lest we be found fighting against God," lest we be guilty of "quenching the Spirit of God."[2]

So far everything has been kept at a nice, safe distance. The Spirit's flame has been burning, but we have not flown so close that we've felt too much heat, right? Oh, we've talked about the Spirit transforming our lives, but mainly we've focused on Jesus and His disciples, an upstairs room in Jerusalem, and the folks who formed the early church. The "tongues of fire" touched them (not us) and the supernatural manifestations were what they (not we) experienced. So everything's been cool.

Until now.

In this chapter, I want to bring *us* into the picture. We're going to be flying a little closer to the flame. But don't worry . . . you're safe.

The Spirit . . . My Sin

In his letter to the Romans, Paul does a masterful job of preparing the reader for his first mention of the Holy Spirit. For almost half the letter, the subject is sin. Sin, sin, and more sin for five consecutive chapters.

When he introduces sin (in the first three chapters), the scene is foul; all hope seems lost. Mankind is wicked to the core, totally depraved, morally adrift, humanly hopeless. Anyone who reads Romans 1–3 and doesn't come to that conclusion has missed the message by a mile.

In Romans 4 and 5, Christ is introduced. Since He has redeemed us from sin's domination, a bright light of hope appears on the horizon. His death at Calvary brought the promise of relief, restored peace with God, and made it possible for God to declare us righteous on the basis of Christ's redeeming work on our behalf. This is known as "justification."

Sin's power was at last diffused, and the bondage was broken—at least theoretically. Sin was not eradicated, but its permanent hold on us was once-for-all released. When the sinner believes in the Lord Jesus Christ, a new Master enters the picture . . . and the old master (the devil) hates it! He called the shots so long, he thinks he is still king of the mountain.

Knowing this to be true, Paul then does major surgery on the subject in the next three chapters. Let me summarize:

• *Romans 6:* Sin no longer has power over us. We have been emancipated. The freedom is ours to claim. Enjoy your liberty, but don't take advantage of it. Since you're free from your old master, don't let sin reign over you any longer. The liberating message of Romans 6 is pretty well capsulized in these two verses:

> Therefore do not let sin reign in your mortal body that you should obey its lusts, and do not go on presenting the members of your body to sin as instruments of unrighteousness; but present yourselves to God as those alive from the dead, and your members as instruments of righteousness to God.
> Romans 6:12–13

• *Romans 7:* But sin is still present within me; I sometimes struggle over who is going to be in charge. I may have been emancipated, but the old master is very much alive . . . and there are times he gives me fits.

Every Christian I know can identify with Paul's honest admission:

> For we know that the Law is spiritual; but I am of flesh, sold into bondage to sin. For that which I am doing, I do not understand; for I am not practicing what I would like to do, but I am doing the very thing I hate.
>
> Romans 7:14–15

You and I may have a new Master, but sin is still there within us, still crouching near the door, ready to pounce! The battle is so relentless, so ruthless, it sometimes gets depressing . . . which may have been the very reason Paul finally let it all out:

> Wretched man that I am! Who will set me free from the body of this death?
>
> Romans 7:24

Great question! Who indeed is able to give me the victory over my old master . . . who indeed will "set me free" from the clawing, clutching, clinging presence of sin?

And we're back to the same magnificent solution: the Transformer Himself—THE HOLY SPIRIT! Which becomes the subject of—

• *Romans 8:* The Spirit provides a new dimension of living. The depressing syndrome set forth in Romans 7 is overcome in Romans 8. The "law of sin and of death" that habitually condemned us in our lost estate has been conquered by "the Spirit of life in Christ Jesus." That is why "There is therefore now no condemnation for those who are in Christ Jesus" (8:1).

Paul deliberately paces himself in the writing of Romans. Chapter after chapter, he deals with sin, sin, and more sin . . . with not one word of relief from the dark side. And then, as the curtain seems to be closing and the reader reaches rock bottom with no way through and no way out . . . Eureka! Enter "the Spirit of life." The curtain quickly reopens, the stage is flooded with light, and the Transformer is introduced. What great writing! Read this grand section of Romans 8 slowly, thoughtfully.

> There is therefore now no condemnation for those who are in Christ Jesus. For the law of the Spirit of life in Christ Jesus has set you free from the law of sin and of death. For what the Law could not do, weak as it was through the flesh, God did: sending His own Son in the likeness of sinful flesh and as an offering for sin, He condemned sin in the flesh, in order that the requirement of the Law might be fulfilled in us, who do not walk according to the flesh, but according to the Spirit. For those who are according to the flesh set their minds on the things of the flesh, but those who are according to the Spirit, the things of the Spirit. For the mind set on the flesh is death, but the mind set on the Spirit is life and peace, because the mind set on the flesh is hostile toward God; for it does not subject itself to the law of God, for it is not even able to do so; and those who are in the flesh cannot please God. However, you are not in the flesh but in the Spirit, if indeed the Spirit of God dwells in you. But if anyone does not have the Spirit of Christ, he does not belong to Him. And if Christ is in you, though the body is dead because of sin, yet the spirit is alive because of righteousness. But if the Spirit of Him who raised Jesus from the dead dwells in you, He who raised Christ Jesus from the dead will also give life to your mortal bodies through His Spirit who indwells you.
>
> So then, brethren, we are under obligation, not to the flesh, to live according to the flesh—for if you are living according to the flesh, you must die; but if by the Spirit you are putting to death the deeds of the body, you will live. For all who are being led by the Spirit of God, these are sons of God.
>
> Romans 8:1–14

Why is the Spirit suddenly introduced in this manner? Because there is no way you or I could curtail and control the fleshly side of our lives apart from Him. But the good news is this: Because He is in us, we can. And because we can . . . we *must!*

My Flesh . . . His Spirit

Since both the Spirit and the flesh are resident within each believer, invariably there is a struggle going on beneath the surface of our lives. Every day we live it is there, simmering on the back burner of our minds. It is like a war in the soul . . . a bloodless battle that won't go away.

This does not mean we're carnal; it means we're human. There is no sin in admitting to the struggle. In fact, if you don't believe such a struggle exists, you haven't been honest with yourself nor have you spent sufficient time in the latter half of Galatians 5.

> But I say, walk by the Spirit, and you will not carry out the desire of the flesh. For the flesh sets its desire against the Spirit, and the Spirit against the flesh; for these are in opposition to one another, so that you may not do the things that you please.
>
> Galatians 5:16–17

To make it even clearer than that, let's look at a paraphrase of verse 17 from The Living Bible:

> For we naturally love to do evil things that are just the opposite from the things that the Holy Spirit tells us to do; and the good things we want to do when the Spirit has his way with us are just the opposite of our natural desires. These two forces within us are constantly fighting each other to win control over us, and our wishes are never free from their pressures.

The Amplified Bible renders the central part of that verse, "these are antagonistic to each other—continually withstanding and in conflict with each other."

Isn't that the truth? Deep within the recesses of our minds there is this invisible, albeit hostile, battleground. On one side are my fleshly desires; on the other, the blessed Spirit of God. One is dark; the other light. One is evil; the other righteous. One is full of lethal drives and desires; the other is nothing but wholesome and healthy.

Because that conflict is carried out in the invisible realm, we seldom think of it in such objective terms, but the contrasts could not be more antithetical. If it were not for the restraining presence of the Spirit, you and I would be the personification of wickedness. No sin would be too extreme. No act of disobedience too rebellious. The darkness of our souls would be blacker than a thousand caverns at midnight. Unrestrained, the flesh knows no bounds within the dark sphere of iniquity.

When the Flesh Is Dominant

Perhaps that may seem exaggerated. Could I have overstated our potential for evil? You decide:

> Now the deeds of the flesh are evident, which are: immorality, impurity, sensuality, idolatry, sorcery, enmities, strife, jealousy, outbursts of anger, disputes, dissensions, factions, envying, drunkenness, carousings, and things like these, of which I forewarn you just as I have forewarned you that those who practice such things shall not inherit the kingdom of God.
> Galatians 5:19–21

Quite a list, isn't it? Looks terribly bleak to me. In fact, it's the same list of sins that could be applied to those outside of Christ. And that's just the point! When God's people traffic in these things, the world cannot tell the difference between *us* and *them*.

Before we go further, perhaps I should clarify the meaning of the phrase, "those who practice such things shall not inherit the kingdom of God."

Paul selects words very carefully. For example, "practice." The tense of the original verb suggests "habitually practice." In other words, it refers to one whose entire life is consumed by such evil. Clearly that is a description of the lifestyle of depraved sinners who have no escape in themselves.

But before we cluck our tongues at those who "habitually practice" such things, let's keep in mind that our old nature remains just as dark and depraved as theirs, even though the Spirit resides within us. Were it not for the presence of God's Spirit, our wickedness would know no bounds.

But He is there . . . He lives within . . . He prompts us to live above the dregs of depravity. Were that not true, we would be hopelessly awash in the activities of the flesh.

When the Spirit Takes Control

The good news is: We don't have to serve the old master any longer! Now that we have our Lord's divine, dynamic presence perpetually living within us, we can live above all that . . . and we can do so on a consistent basis. By the Spirit's filling, evidences of our new nature emerge.

So what occurs? What, for example, is produced when the Spirit is in full control? Paul answers that question directly.

> But the fruit of the Spirit is love, joy, peace, patience, kindness, goodness, faithfulness, gentleness, self-control; against such things there is no law.
>
> Galatians 5:22–23

And that is just a brief sampling of what He produces within us. Magnificent thought! By turning the controls of our life over to Him who lives within, we begin to model the life Christ modeled when He lived and walked on earth. When that happens, the transformation process kicks in.

The choice is ours. Remember Romans 8:5?

> For those who are according to the flesh set their minds on the things of the flesh, but those who are according to the Spirit, the things of the Spirit.

For years I wondered what "the things of the Spirit" were. Now I know!

We can produce "the things of the flesh" by setting our mind on such . . . or we can produce "the things of the Spirit" by giving Him control of our life. It's that simple. We become the followers of whichever master we choose to obey. That is precisely what Paul wrote to the first-century Christians in Rome:

> Do you not know that when you present yourselves to someone as slaves for obedience, you are slaves of the one whom you obey, either of sin resulting in death, or of obedience resulting in righteousness?
>
> Romans 6:16

Living under the control of our flesh is a deathlike existence. We are miserable, feel guilty and ashamed, and the emptiness within is worse than bad. But when we are operating under the dominating influence of the Spirit, "the things of the Spirit" are reproduced in us and through us.

And what are some of them? Romans 8 leaves us with quite a list.

• *Life and peace.*

> For the mind set on the flesh is death, but the mind set on the Spirit is life and peace.
>
> Romans 8:6

• *Absence of fear and closeness to God.*

> For you have not received a spirit of slavery leading to fear again, but you have received a spirit of adoption as sons by which we cry out, "Abba! Father!"
>
> Romans 8:15

• *Inner assurance . . . doubts gone!*

> The Spirit Himself bears witness with our spirit that we are children of God, and if children, heirs also, heirs of God and fellow heirs with Christ, if indeed we suffer with Him in order that we may also be glorified with Him
>
> Romans 8:16–17

And in the same way the Spirit also helps our weakness; for we do not know how to pray as we should, but the Spirit Himself intercedes for us with groanings too deep for words; and He who searches the hearts knows what the mind of the Spirit is, because He intercedes for the saints according to the will of God.

Romans 8:26–27

• *Inner awareness that "all things" are working together for good and God's glory.*

And we know that God causes all things to work together for good to those who love God, to those who are called according to His purpose.

Romans 8:28

Leaving Room for Mystery

When Jesus and Nicodemus met one night to discuss spiritual things, the Lord gave the inquiring Pharisee—and us—a lot to think about, including statements about the flesh and the Spirit. At one point He said:

"The wind blows where it wishes and you hear the sound of it, but do not know where it comes from and where it is going; so is every one who is born of the Spirit."

John 3:8

Normally we apply that statement to salvation, meaning that the Spirit moves silently, mysteriously, and unexpectedly, prompting various individuals to turn to Christ and be born again. That is true, but I suggest that Jesus' words also indicate that the Spirit continues to move like the wind that blows. How silently and how mysteriously He works within us! In unexpected and spontaneous ways, He works out God's perfect and profound will.

How unsearchable are His judgments and unfathomable His ways!

Romans 11:33

We are unwise to restrict the workings of the Spirit to one simplistic system we feel we can analyze and explain. Let's not do that! Let's not try to box Him in.

Remember . . . He is like the wind . . . mysteriously on the move . . . blowing here, changing there, altering plans, creating stretching situations, stimulating wholesome desires, prompting decisions. These are all included in "the things of the Spirit," and only those who fly closer to the flame are sensitive enough to realize that.

So? Move closer. Don't be afraid. Be open and willing to let fresh wonder in. Leave plenty of room for the Spirit to work . . . to move . . . to reveal . . . to bring new dimensions of freedom. Paul experienced this, as he admits to his friends in Corinth:

> But just as it is written,
>
> > "THINGS WHICH EYE HAS NOT SEEN AND
> >   EAR HAS NOT HEARD,
> > AND WHICH HAVE NOT ENTERED THE
> >   HEART OF MAN,
> > ALL THAT GOD HAS PREPARED FOR THOSE
> >   WHO LOVE HIM."
>
> For to us God revealed them through the Spirit; for the Spirit searches all things, even the depths of God. For who among men knows the thoughts of a man except the spirit of the man, which is in him? Even so the thoughts of God no one knows except the Spirit of God. Now we have received, not the spirit of the world, but the Spirit who is from God, that we might know the things freely given to us by God, which things we also speak, not in words taught by human wisdom, but in those taught by the Spirit, combining spiritual thoughts with spiritual words.
>
> 1 Corinthians 2:9–13

Of special interest to me here is that unusual comment he makes regarding how "the Spirit searches all things, even the depths of God." As we plumb those "depths" by means of the Spirit, we discover many of "the things freely given to us by God."

Such "things" do not enter our conscious minds so long as sin dominates. But when we are filled with the Spirit (we'll look at that in detail in the next chapter), our minds and hearts are open to spiritual dimensions we never knew existed and we begin to be truly transformed.

Three Absolutely Thrilling Thoughts

Let me leave you with three thoughts God gave me as I wrote this chapter. After reading each one, close your eyes and allow the words to sink into your mind.

- There are realms of earthly experience we have never traveled. (As we fly closer to the flame, the Spirit can open them up to us.)

  Pause and think it over . . .

- There are depths of God's will we have never tapped. (As we fly closer to the flame, the Spirit can reveal them to us.)

  Pause and think it over . . .

- There are dimensions of supernatural power we have never touched. (As we fly closer to the flame, the Spirit will allow that to happen.)

  Pause and think it over . . .

4

Is the Spirit's Filling That Big a Deal?

*H*AVE YOU EVER SENSED the need for an acute awareness of the Spirit of God? I have, as I'm sure you have. For most of us those times come wrapped in various packages:

- We face some awful trial from which we cannot escape.
- A physician tells us he is concerned about the x-rays.
- The telephone rings in the middle of the night, leaving us reeling over news of some tragedy.
- We need to know God's will in an important matter, which could lead to life-changing results.
- We are the target of an attack that becomes complicated and ugly.

On such occasions worry kicks in, our stomach churns, our head spins. We get the jitters. We feel the beginning stages of panic. We need help . . . and not the kind someone else can provide.

We need God. We need Him to step in, calm our fears, and take charge. More than all that, we need the confidence that He is there at that very moment. It's not that we expect an audible voice from heaven or a moving-picture vision of the future in Technicolor. Not that. What we need most is that inner reassurance that He is there, that He cares, that He is in full control.

Some years ago my phone rang in the middle of the day on a Friday. It was someone from our older daughter's school telling me that Charissa had been in an accident. She had been practicing a pyramid formation with her cheerleading squad when someone at the bottom slipped, causing the whole human pyramid to collapse. Charissa had been at the top and, consequently, fell the farthest, hitting the back of her head with a sharp jolt. Her legs and arms had gone numb, and she was unable to move even her fingers. After notifying the paramedics, the school official had called me.

My wife, Cynthia, was away at the time, so I raced to the school alone, not knowing what I'd find or how serious our daughter had been injured. En route, I prayed aloud. I called out to the Lord like a child trapped in an empty well. I told Him I would need Him for several things: to touch my daughter, to give me strength, to provide skill and wisdom to the paramedics. Tears were near the surface, so I asked Him to calm me, to restrain the growing sense of panic within me.

As I drove and prayed, I sensed the most incredible realization of God's presence. It was almost eerie. The pulse that had been thumping in my throat returned to normal. When I reached the school parking lot, even the swirling red and blue lights atop the emergency vehicle didn't faze my sense of calm.

I ran to where the crowd had gathered. By that time the paramedics had Charissa wrapped tightly on a stretcher, her neck in a brace. I knelt beside her, kissed her on the forehead, and heard her say, "I can't feel anything below my shoulders. Something snapped in my back, just below my neck." She was blinking through tears.

Normally, I would have been borderline out of control. I wasn't. Normally, I would have been shouting for the crowd to back away or for the ambulance driver to get her to the hospital immediately! I didn't. With remarkable ease, I stroked the hair away from her eyes and whispered, "I'm here with you, sweetheart. So is our Lord. No matter what happens, we'll make it through this together. I love you, Charissa." Tears ran down the side of her face as she closed her eyes.

Calmly, I stood and spoke with the emergency medical personnel. We agreed on which hospital she should go to and what route we would take. I followed in my car, again sensing the

Spirit's profound and sovereign presence. Cynthia joined me at the hospital, where we waited for the x-rays and the radiologist's report. We prayed, and I told her of my encounter with the Spirit's wonderful presence.

In a few hours we learned that a vertebrae in Charissa's back had been fractured. The doctors did not know how much damage had been done to the nerves as a result of the fall and fracture. Neither did they know how long it would take for the numbness to subside or if, in fact, it would. The physicians were careful with their words, and I can still remember how grim both of them seemed. We had nothing tangible to rely on, nothing medical to count on, and nothing emotional to lean on . . . except the Spirit of God, who had stayed with us through the entire ordeal.

Sunday was just around the corner (it always is). I was exhausted by Saturday night, but again God's Spirit remained my stability. In human weakness and with enormous dependence, I preached on Sunday morning. The Lord gave me the words, and He proved His strength in my weakness. (I am told by our audio tape department that that particular message remains one of the most requested sermons on tape of all the messages I've delivered since I first became pastor of the church back in 1971.)

Amazing! God the Holy Spirit filled me, took full control, gave great grace, calmed fears, and ultimately brought wonderful healing to Charissa's back. Today she is a healthy, happy wife and mother of two, and the only time her upper back hurts is when she sneezes! When that happens and I'm with her, I usually look at her and ask, "Did that hurt?" Invariably, she nods and says, "Yeah, it did." I smile, she smiles back, and for a moment we mentally return to that original scene where she and I felt a very real awareness of the Spirit's presence.

The Christian life is a life lived on a spiritual plane—a realm that includes dimensions foreign to those who are non-Christians. To them, such scenes as I have just described are unreal and borderline unacceptable. A better word is foolish. That's understandable, since they haven't the Spirit within them. Remember what Paul wrote the Corinthians?

But a natural man does not accept the things of the Spirit of God; for they are foolishness to him, and he cannot understand them, because they are spiritually appraised.

1 Corinthians 2:14

The Greek term translated "foolishness" is *moros,* from which we get "moronic." That fits. To the skeptical unbeliever, "the things of the Spirit" are totally stupid, absolutely ridiculous. A waste of time. But to us who understand how to operate in a world where things are "spiritually appraised," it is remarkable how much goes on in that dimension. In fact, let's return to some spiritual "basics."

Christianity 101

To enter the Christian life, a person must begin at the right place: conversion. That means we must be rightly related to the Lord Jesus Christ. No matter what our background may be, regardless of name, sex, status, language, color, or culture, everyone begins the Christian life the same way: by coming to Christ in faith, accepting His sacrifice on the cross as sufficient payment for sin.

Jesus said to him, "I am the way, and the truth, and the life; no one comes to the Father, but through Me.

John 14:6

For by grace you have been saved through faith; and that not of yourselves, it is the gift of God; not as a result of works, that no one should boast.

Ephesians 2:8–9

And the witness is this, that God has given us eternal life, and this life is in His Son. He who has the Son has the life; he who does not have the Son of God does not have the life.

1 John 5:11–12

Then, to live the Christian life, a person must continue under the control of the right power—the power of the Holy Spirit.

To enter these new dimensions of the spiritual life, we must be rightly related to the Holy Spirit.

> As you therefore have received Christ Jesus the Lord, so walk in Him.
>
> Colossians 2:6

We become Christians because we "received Christ Jesus the Lord." We become empowered and filled with the Spirit as we "walk in Him."

Both are essential if we hope to enjoy all the benefits of the Christian life, for it is possible to be converted and yet not live on a spiritual plane. It is one thing to become a Christian. It is another thing entirely to become a Spirit-filled Christian. The tragedy is that so many are converted and so few Spirit-filled. When this happens, a person misses the best God has to offer us on earth.

What fuel is to a car, the Holy Spirit is to the believer. He energizes us to stay the course. He motivates us in spite of the obstacles. He keeps us going when the road gets rough. It is the Spirit who comforts us in our distress, who calms us in times of calamity, who becomes our companion in loneliness and grief, who spurs our "intuition" into action, who fills our minds with discernment when we are uneasy about a certain decision. In short, He is our spiritual fuel. When we attempt to operate without Him or to use some substitute fuel, all systems grind to a halt.

A Necessary Reminder of Who—and Whose—We Are

While the fuel and the car may help illustrate salvation and spirituality, it breaks down (no pun intended) at one important point. We own our car; we don't own ourselves. We have been purchased by another, and the price was Jesus' death on the cross. Jesus' blood was payment in full for our sins.

> Or do you not know that your body is a temple of the Holy Spirit who is in you, whom you have from God, and that you

are not your own? For you have been bought with a price: therefore glorify God in your body.

1 Corinthians 6:19–20

We do not belong to ourselves, nor should we operate independently of the Spirit of God. Now that we have been converted, we are the Lord's, and as our Master, He has every right to use us in whatever way He chooses. In living out the Christian life, we have one major objective: to "glorify God in [our] body."

Since the believer's body is considered the "temple of the Holy Spirit," it stands to reason that He should be glorified in it and through it. He owns it! This completely rearranges our reason for existence. When you operate your life from this perspective, it changes everything. That explains why it is so important to view every day—sunup to sundown—from the spiritual dimension. When we do, nothing is accidental, coincidental, meaningless, or superficial. Things that happen to us are under our Lord's supervision because we are His, and we are to glorify Him, regardless. Since we belong to Him and His Spirit lives in us, we are in good hands. We occupy, in fact, the best possible situation on earth.

This means that words like "accidents" or "coincidences" should be removed from our vocabulary. Seriously! When events transpire that we cannot understand or explain, we are reminded that we are not our own. Rather than being upset, frustrated, or confused, we need to allow His Spirit to fill us with the divine fuel we need to serve Him and honor Him in those events—to glorify Him.

Let me remind you that as a Christian, you have the Holy Spirit. You don't need to pray for Him to come into your life; He's already there. He came to reside within you when you were converted, even though you may not have known it. Remember how Paul put it in the verses we just considered?

Or do you not know that your body is a temple of the Holy Spirit who is in you, *whom you have from God?*" (italics mine).

1 Corinthians 6:19

A little later on in the same letter, we are told that we have been "baptized" by the Spirit into the universal "body" of Christ. Read these words slowly and carefully:

> For by one Spirit we were all baptized into one body, whether Jews or Greeks, whether slaves or free, and we were all made to drink of one Spirit.
>
> 1 Corinthians 12:13

Every child of God has been "identified" with and made a part of the body. Never question that again! Romans 8:9 says the same thing in different words:

> But if anyone does not have the Spirit of Christ, he does not belong to Him.

Establish this dual truth once and for all: If you are a Christian, you have the Spirit living within you at all times; if you are not a Christian, you do not have the Spirit.

The wonderful part of all this is that by having the Spirit, you and I have all the "fuel" we need. Since He indwells us, He is there, ready to energize us and empower us at any time.

When I got that phone call about my daughter, I didn't ask God to "send Your Holy Spirit . . . I need Him with me to strengthen and stabilize me." No, I acknowledged that He was already there, and I consciously engaged the gears that gave Him full control. Why? Because I wanted to "glorify God" in the midst of the events that were transpiring. So I asked Him to fill me with fresh and dynamic power . . . which He did.

An Essential Revelation of What We Have

Even though every believer has the Holy Spirit, it is possible to operate our lives apart from His control. But when that happens—which it does with many Christians every day—what is missed is nothing short of tragic. When we operate under His control, the potential for peace and joy, calm and comfort, guidance and insight, confidence and courage know no bounds. That is not an exaggeration; it is fact. This is why an understanding of the filling of the Spirit is absolutely crucial.

How Are We Filled with the Spirit?

To return to my analogy, our tank is full. We need no more fuel, nor should we attempt to use a substitute fuel. We, as believers, have all the fuel that is needed for all the power, insight, comfort, guidance, courage, and dynamic we will ever need. The question is, How do we get the fuel flowing so we can operate our lives as God intended? Or, to use the scriptural terms, How are we filled with the Spirit? Is there a certain technique?

Let's examine the primary biblical reference on the filling of the Holy Spirit, Ephesians 5, which begins:

> Therefore be imitators of God, as beloved children; and walk in love, just as Christ also loved you, and gave Himself up for us, an offering and a sacrifice to God as a fragrant aroma . . . for you were formerly darkness, but now you are light in the Lord; walk as children of light.
>
> Ephesians 5:1–2, 8

Ephesians 5 begins with three strong commands:

- "be imitators of God"
- "walk in love"
- "walk as children of light."

Clearly, the Christian life is a life that honors God and demonstrates Christlikeness. Those who "imitate God" do both as they walk in love and walk in light. No wonder we are warned:

> Therefore be careful how you walk, not as unwise men, but as wise. . . . So then do not be foolish, but understand what the will of the Lord is.
>
> Ephesians 5:15, 17

What is that "will of God"? We are told clearly and succinctly in the next verse:

> And do not get drunk with wine, for that is dissipation, but be filled with the Spirit.
>
> Ephesians 5:18

Interestingly, in the Scriptures we are never commanded to "Be baptized in the Spirit!" or "Be indwelt by the Spirit!" or "Be gifted!" or "Be sealed!" But here in a context of various commands, we are clearly commanded to "Be filled with the Spirit!" Therefore, it is something we are to obey. In fact, there are two commands. The first is *negative:* "do not get drunk with wine"; and the second is *positive:* "but be filled with the Spirit."

I have heard it taught that these two ought to be combined in some way. For example, some say that the fullness of the Spirit is like spiritual inebriation . . . like a "divine intoxication." It's as if the believer is virtually out of control under the influence of the Spirit. When "drunk with wine," a person is physically filled with alcohol; when "drunk in the Spirit," one is spiritually allied with Him.

I question this interpretation, given the context. This verse is not comparing the two; it is offering them as contrasts to one another. This is emphasized by Paul's adding that drunkenness "is dissipation," which means debauchery, excess, existing hopelessly out of control. But the Spirit-filled Christian is never "out of control." On the contrary, you may recall that among the list of the fruit of the Spirit is *self-control* (Galatians 5:23). Rather than likening these two, I suggest it is better to contrast them. As John R. W. Stott correctly observes:

> We can indeed agree that in both drunkenness and the fullness of the Spirit two strong influences are at work within us, alcohol in the bloodstream and the Holy Spirit in our hearts. But, whereas excessive alcohol leads to unrestrained and irrational licence, transforming the drunkard into an animal,

the fullness of the Spirit leads to restrained and rational moral behaviour, transforming the Christian into the image of Christ. Thus, the results of being under the influence of spirits on the one hand and of the Holy Spirit of God on the other are totally and utterly different. One makes us like beasts, the other like Christ.[1]

Since the climax of Paul's argument is reached in his command regarding the filling of the Spirit, let's probe deeper. Stay with me . . . and you will soon see what good sense this makes.

I am indebted to Dr. Stott for four very helpful observations regarding this crucial verse of Scripture:[2]

First, *the command is in the imperative mood:* "You BE FILLED with the Spirit!" This is no casual, polite, calm suggestion, but a firm, straightforward command. We have no more freedom to ignore this duty than we do to overlook the ethical commands that surround it, such as "work hard," "speak the truth," "be kind," "forgive." You see, "be filled with the Spirit" is like all those other commands. So, Christian, let me admonish you to obey God's strong command. The imperative mood demands obedience!

Second, *the verb "be filled" is in the plural form.* The apostle Paul is not directing this to one special group of people or one superspiritual saint in the church at Ephesus or, for that matter, to the church in general. He is saying to all of us—individually and collectively—that we, as a universal body of Christians, must be filled with the Spirit of God.

Third, *it is in the passive voice.* Did you notice that? "Be filled" is the command, not "Fill yourself up with the Spirit." Or, as The New English Bible renders it: "Let the Holy Spirit fill you." But don't make too much of that. Just as a person gets drunk by drinking alcohol, so an individual is filled with the Spirit by involving himself or herself in the process that leads to it.

For example, I cannot be filled with the Spirit while I have known and unconfessed sin present within me. I cannot be filled with the Spirit while at the same time conducting my life in the energy of the flesh. I cannot be filled with the Spirit while I am walking against God's will and depending upon myself. I need to be sure that I have taken care of the sins that have emerged in my life, that I have not ignored the wrong that I have done before God and to others. I need to walk in dependence on the Lord on a daily basis. Jesus emphasizes the same thought in John 15, where He commands us to abide in the vine. Why? Because "apart from Me you can do nothing" (15:5). And when Jesus says nothing, He means *nothing*.

Many a morning I begin my day by sitting on the side of the bed and saying:

> This is Your day, Lord. I want to be at Your disposal. I have no idea what these next twenty-four hours will contain. But before I begin, before I sip my first cup of coffee, and even before I get dressed, I want You to know that from this moment on throughout this day, I'm Yours, Lord. Help me to be a branch that abides in the vine, to lean on You, to draw strength from You, and to have You fill my mind and my thoughts. Take control of my senses so that I am literally filled with Your presence and power and dynamic. I want to be Your tool, Your vessel today. I can't make it happen. Without You I can accomplish nothing. And so I'm saying, Lord, fill me with Your Spirit today.

Since it works for me, I suggest you give it a try.

Fourth, *the command to "be filled" is in the present tense.* It is a continuous appropriation, not some great high-and-mighty, once-in-a-lifetime moment where you experience the fullness of the Spirit and from then on you are on an all-time high that never wanes. Instead, we are regularly to pray, "Fill me, Lord, for this moment . . . fill me in this hour . . . fill me as I'm facing this challenge."

It's like we are saying, "Lord, I want to be filled. I want to be used. I want to be available. I deliberately and consciously make myself dependent upon You."

The Spirit's filling is like walking. When we are little, every tiny step is a conscious effort and a magnificent achievement. Soon, we learn to link two or three steps together before we fall. And then before you know it, by the time we've reached four or five, we're walking and not even thinking about it. Walking has simply become a part of life.

Over time, as we experience His filling, it becomes a constant part of our consciousness and our life. But we begin deliberately, slowly, and carefully. As the sun tips its hat in the early morning, we say to the Lord: "Lord this is Your day. As these hours unfold, I want to walk with You, allowing Your Spirit full control. Since I belong to You and no day is a waste, help me live it under Your empowering authority."

Now, please be careful. I know as I write this that I have engineer-types reading my words. And engineer-types love techniques. They love a step-by-step, logical process. They love details. Like, "Okay, every step, Lord, this is for You (step 1). And, Lord, may I be filled with the Spirit. And, Lord, this is Your day (step 2). So, Lord, help me with . . . (step 3)."

But the walk of faith by the Spirit's filling isn't mechanical. Instead, it's as if we're saying:

> I am in the process, Lord, of fulfilling Your will. I want to glorify Your name. I belong to You. I pledge my allegiance to You today. Enable me in my walk to have the discernment to walk in obedience and not in disobedience, to sense wrong when I encounter it and to stay away from it. Keep me strong when temptations come. Guard my tongue from saying the wrong thing or saying too much or speaking too quickly. Enable me to restrain profanity and resist outbursts of anger. Lord, help me in my walk. Fill me with Your Spirit. Take my eyes, take my tongue, take my emotions, take my will, and use me, Lord, because I want to be under Your control on a continuing basis.

This is called the Christian walk.

What Happens When We Are Filled with the Spirit?

So now we're ready for the next crucial question: What happens when I am filled with the Spirit? In Ephesians 5, after the command to "be filled with the Spirit," we are told of four results in the Christian's life.

> . . . be filled with the Spirit, speaking to one another in psalms and hymns and spiritual songs, singing and making melody with your heart to the Lord; always giving thanks for all things in the name of our Lord Jesus Christ to God, even the Father; and be subject to one another in the fear of Christ.
>
> Ephesians 5:18–21

First, *His filling affects our speaking.* To begin with, we are "speaking to one another." This is a vital part of what is called Christian fellowship. Or, as Paul puts it in his letter to the Colossians:

> Let the word of Christ richly dwell within you, with all wisdom teaching and admonishing one another with psalms and hymns and spiritual songs, singing with thankfulness in your hearts to God. And whatever you do in word or deed, do all in the name of the Lord Jesus, giving thanks through Him to God the Father.
>
> Colossians 3:16–17

When we are filled with the Spirit, we begin to relate to others in the family of God. We want to hear what they have to say. We want to learn from one another. And we also want to contribute to each other's welfare. If we see our brothers and sisters in a dangerous or perilous situation, we want to warn them.

Second, *His filling leads us to melodious hearts.* We not only speak to one another; we live in harmony with one another.

> . . . in psalms and hymns and spiritual songs, singing and making melody with your heart to God.
>
> Ephesians 5:19

Life takes on a special lilt. Joy comes again.

As he leads our worship and serves as music pastor at our church, Howie Stevenson frequently exhorts us to do what we do "heartily." It's one of his favorite expressions. And it's an appropriate biblical word, for the Spirit's filling opens our hearts and moves us into an enthusiastic overflow of worship.

One of the characteristics of Spirit-filled believers is that they don't wait until Sunday to worship. They have a daily worship occurring in their lives. We may be singers. We may not be singers. (Or at least we don't sing in public!) But all of us can have an inner melody that bubbles up spontaneously out of our lives. And I have observed that when I am walking in the Spirit there is usually a song on the tip of my tongue because there is a melody flowing through my heart. There is, even in a broader sense, a desire to live in harmony with my brothers and sisters.

Third, *His filling makes us thankful people.*

> . . . always giving thanks for all things in the name of our
> Lord Jesus Christ to God, even the Father.
> Ephesians 5:20

One of the telltale signs of the Spirit-filled life is gratitude. Show me a grumbler, and I'll show you a person who has distanced herself or himself from the Spirit of God. When we are filled with the Spirit, there is an overwhelming sense of thankfulness. We are not hard to please. We are happy to have whatever God provides. We're not spoiled or "choosy."

Fourth, *His filling leads us to submit to each other.*

> . . . and be subject to one another in the fear of Christ.
> Ephesians 5:21

When we are filled with the Spirit, we become more submissive to those in our lives.

If we are in leadership, a servant-hearted style replaces a demanding, dogmatic style. A God-directed humility emerges.

If we are married, our Spirit-filled heart prompts us to want to serve our mates, not control them. Difficult though it may be for some dominant male types to accept, in marriage there is to be a mutual submission to one another, a teachability, an openness. Not only for the wife toward her husband, but for the husband toward his wife.

> Husbands, love your wives, just as Christ also loved the church and gave Himself up for her.
>
> Ephesians 5:25

Just as Christ loved the church, the Spirit-filled husband loves his wife. Submission is not a one-way street.

Recently I heard Jack Hayford tell about a married couple who had attended a seminar taught by one of those male demagogues determined to show that Scripture teaches that the man is IN CHARGE at home. It was the kind of terrible teaching on submission that turns women into lowly doormats. Well, the husband just loved it! He had never heard anything like it in his life, and he drank it all in. His wife, however, sat there fuming as she listened to hour after hour of this stuff.

When they left the meeting that night, the husband felt drunk with fresh power as he climbed into the car. While driving home, he said rather pompously, "Well, what did you think about that?" His wife didn't utter a word . . . so he continued, "I think it was *great!*"

When they arrived home, she got out and followed him silently into the house. Once inside, he slammed the door and said, "Wait right there . . . just stand right there." She stood, tight-lipped, and stared at him. "I've been thinking about what that fellow said tonight, and I want you to know that from now on *that's* the way it's gonna be around here. You got it? *That's* the way things are gonna run in this house!"

And having said that, he didn't see her for two weeks. After two weeks, *he could start to see her just a little bit out of one eye.*

I have discovered over the years that there is something really twisted in the mind of a man who thinks that submission is limited to the woman. I have also discovered that there is seldom a problem with submission in the home when a husband has a heart that is genuinely submissive to God. The reason is clear: With a heart submissive to God, the Spirit-filled man truly loves his wife as Christ loved the church . . . there's no one else on earth he loves quite like her. And he demonstrates it by listening when she speaks . . . by respecting her opinion . . . by caring for her . . . by releasing many of his own rights. Part of love is sharing. When a wife knows that she is enveloped in that kind of respectful affection, she has no trouble at all yielding to her husband.

The Spirit-filled walk will not only change a life; in the process it absolutely transforms a home.

A Practical Response to How We Live

Let me conclude by reminding you once again that we do not need to plead for God's presence. We have it. We don't need to spend our days wondering why some people have an edge on the power. We have it too. We don't need to toss and turn through sleepless nights, struggling over our inability to claim the same superdynamic power that some televangelist seems to have and we don't. Let me repeat, as a Christian you have the Spirit of God.

But even though this is true, several probing questions are in order:

- Are you engaging the gears?
- Are you keeping short accounts on those things that break fellowship with God?
- Are you walking in conscious dependence on the Lord?
- Are you saying to Him at the beginning of—and frequently throughout—the day, "Lord, my life is Yours"?

Finally, I want to close with three important reminders to believers regarding the Spirit-filled life.

First, *abnormal experiences are not necessary to Christian maturity.*

Some groups in the evangelical community place a great deal of emphasis on phenomenal, exceptional manifestations of the Spirit. Others find themselves uncomfortable with this type of expression; they may even feel that it can't be defended from the Scriptures. Let me encourage you, whatever your frame of reference, to be gracious, be tolerant.

As a matter of fact, I would pass on to you the advice of Gamaliel, who gave this counsel to his friends as they were wondering what to do with the apostles who were turning the world upside down:

> "And so in the present case, I say to you, stay away from these men and let them alone, for if this plan or action should be of men, it will be overthrown; but if it is of God, you will not be able to overthrow them; or else you may even be found fighting against God."
>
> Acts 5:38–39

So my plea to those whose particular persuasion does not happen to fit a particular expression of the fullness of the Spirit (I'm trying to stay away from all the labels), be tolerant of those for whom it is.

When I was fresh out of seminary, I felt it necessary to correct all the things that I didn't agree with. I felt it necessary to be the self-appointed crusader and to address all those expressions of the faith that did not coincide with my convictions. But over the years I have found that that is a great way to waste a lot of energy. God did not call me to clean up the entire world (which, being interpreted, means to straighten others out so they would get in step with my convictions), I have learned over the years to be a lot more tolerant and a little wiser.

Second, *the fullness of the Spirit is for all of us, as believers, to enjoy, but how it works its way out in each person's life is another matter.*

So for those who place a great deal of emphasis on the supernatural, remember: Rejoice in the comfort He has brought you in your walk, but don't try to force your experience upon everyone else. Don't feel you must be a zealous proselyte for your convictions, and don't stereotype all Christian experiences. You will blend a lot more easily into the body of Christ and you will find a great deal more satisfaction in your walk with the Lord if you will simply accept that as your own personal experience. But please don't look down your nose as though you have something that others don't have which makes you especially spiritual.

Let's live comfortably with each other and with our experiential differences . . . even different expressions of the fullness of the Spirit.

Third, *let us seek to enjoy our vast common ground, rather than establish and defend our own theological turf.*

I have said for years that there are more things that draw us together than there are things that separate us. We should be enjoying the vast common ground of our faith rather than defending some particular area of theological or experiential persuasion. Relax. You take care of your responsibilities before the Lord and let your brothers and sisters take care of theirs. Let's allow God to be God and understand that we are all in His family.

Shortly after his conversion in 1929, C. S. Lewis wrote this note to a friend: "When all is said (and truly said) about divisions of Christendom, there remains, by God's mercy, an enormous common ground."[3]

Since the common ground is so enormous, I suggest that we ask the Spirit of God to give us "enormous tolerance" with one another, which includes great joy in His presence, so that we do not feel the need to get everybody to walk in lockstep with us.

There was a time in my Christian life when if I heard a person say some of the things I've been suggesting, I would probably have labeled him or her a quasi-heretic—you know, soft, not really a person of conviction. But I don't feel that now. I've come to realize that God not only uses a whole lot of people, He uses some I don't even particularly like. And to the surprise of those who don't really like me that much, I, too, am being used. While we may be small-minded, our Father is not. He delights in blessing the full spectrum of His people in innumerable ways.

Aren't you glad that we are not God? Aren't you glad that our loving Father, who is the source of our fuel and our reason for existence, is still on the throne and is still committed to using each one of us for His glory?

May our "enormous common ground" be the foundation that supports us, rather than a battlefield that separates. The secret for making that happen? The filling of the Spirit . . . nothing more, nothing less, nothing else.

> *Spirit of the living God, fall afresh on me!*
> *Be honored in my submissive spirit.*
> *Be seen and heard in my melodious heart.*
> *Be observed in my thankfulness.*
> *Be glorified in the fellowship and worship that I have with*
>   *others in Your family.*

5

The Spirit Who Surprises

I HAVE JUST EXPERIENCED ONE of the greatest surprises of my life. Certainly, it is *the* greatest surprise in more than twenty years of my life. Looking back on the whole thing, I now realize it was the Spirit of God who orchestrated every one of the events. My head is still swimming. I'm certain that my pulse won't return to normal for several more days.

I have accepted the invitation from my alma mater, Dallas Theological Seminary, to become its next president. In all candor, I am still trying to believe it, especially since I was so firmly convinced thirteen months ago that I should *not* say yes. In fact, when asked to reconsider my decision six months later, I was even more convinced I was not the one for the job. So, after giving myself more time to think it through, I said no again, only this time with greater assurance than before. I even requested that the presidential search committee accept my no as absolutely final. I was convinced beyond all doubt.

And then the Spirit took over.

I'll not attempt to spell out all the details of what transpired, who was involved, or how my thinking was changed. But I can assure you that there was one surprise after another: an unexpected conversation that proved to be what I would call an attention-grabber . . . an unpredictable suggestion at just the right time, which made it impossible to ignore . . . an individual who challenged me to look at the picture in a completely different way . . . and then one person after another (plus one significant group of people after another) who affirmed the idea and encouraged me to accept the position.

And so here I sit, only hours removed from a whirlwind of activities connected with my accepting the school's offer. It will be an unusual arrangement (another of the Spirit's many surprises), whereby I will remain a pastor of a local church, yet still be free to provide the vision, direction, and motivation for the seminary. My plan is to be on hand as much as possible through the year to touch and influence the lives of those in training for a lifetime of ministry. And because of the gifts, diligence, willingness, and competence of a man who will come aboard with me as the provost of the school—Dr. John Sailhamer—I will not have to concern myself with all the time-consuming and energy-draining details that normally sap the strength and blur the vision of a school's president.

Only time will tell how well all this will work, but today I am still shaking my head in amazement. When I realize how full of surprises our God really is, a fresh burst of excitement rushes through me. He has many such things in mind for all of us. If you do not believe that, you are in for a massive surprise! The geography and the details of His plan will be different for each one of us, of course, but the Spirit's sovereign working is far beyond what the human mind can ever imagine. That is precisely what the prophet meant when he wrote:

> "For My thoughts are not your thoughts,
> Neither are your ways My ways," declares the LORD.
> "For as the heavens are higher than the earth,
> So are My ways higher than your ways,
> And My thoughts than your thoughts."
> Isaiah 55:8–9

The problem with most of us is not that our theology is heretical, but that it has become predictable, which, to me, is a synonym for dull and boring. It was never meant to be. The One whom our Lord Jesus sent is the life-giving, always-energizing Spirit, who wants to work in us in phenomenal ways so that we are able to tap the unfathomable depths of God. But the tragedy is that far too many of God's people would rather leave such thoughts safely etched on the pages of Scripture than experience them in practical ways in everyday life.

A Reminder of What Jesus Promised

We have already looked at Jesus' promise to send the Spirit, but maybe it would help to review those words once again:

> "And I will ask the Father, and He will give you another Helper, that He may be with you forever; that is the Spirit of truth, whom the world cannot receive, because it does not behold Him or know Him, but you know Him because He abides with you, and will be in you. . . .
>
> "These things I have spoken to you, while abiding with you. But the Helper, the Holy Spirit, whom the Father will send in My name, He will teach you all things, and bring to your remembrance all that I said to you."
>
> John 14:16–17, 25–26

Twice the term *Helper* is used by our Lord in this section. That word is translated into English from a combination of two Greek terms, *para* (alongside) and *kaleo* (to call). The One whom our Lord will "call alongside" for the purpose of giving us assistance will specifically carry out dual functions. Did you observe them as you read Jesus' promise?

1. He will teach "all things."
2. He will "bring to your remembrance" what Jesus has said.

In other words, it is the Lord's desire to disclose truth rather than hide it and to have us remember rather than forget. Think of it this way: God wants us to know His will so we can walk in it and experience the full manifestations of His power, His blessings. He isn't running away and hiding the pearls of His promises or the gems of His wisdom. No, He has given us His Spirit to reveal those things to us . . . to remind us again and again that Jesus' words are both reliable and true. As we grasp the reality of those things, we are often surprised, since they are so different from what we expect.

An Often-Overlooked Ministry of the Spirit

Shortly before He was arrested and crucified, Jesus made this important prediction and promise. Read it very carefully.

> "But I tell you the truth, it is to your advantage that I go away; for if I do not go away, the Helper shall not come to you; but if I go, I will send Him to you. And He, when He comes, will convict the world concerning sin, and righteousness, and judgment; concerning sin, because they do not believe in Me; and concerning righteousness, because I go to the Father, and you no longer behold Me; and concerning judgment, because the ruler of this world has been judged. "I have many more things to say to you, but you cannot bear them now. But when He, the Spirit of truth, comes, He will guide you into all the truth; for He will not speak on His own initiative, but whatever He hears, He will speak; and He will disclose to you what is to come.
>
> John 16:7–13

Exactly what is it Jesus predicts? He assures us the Spirit will do for us what we cannot do for ourselves. But of special interest to me is His concluding comment. After telling us what the Spirit of God will do regarding sin, righteousness, and judgment, He makes a sweeping prediction most of us have never accepted at face value; namely, "He will guide you into all the truth." Imagine!

For years I embraced a limited view of that statement, even though Jesus specifically used the word "all." I felt He was referring only to the truth of Scripture. That certainly would be included in the category of "the truth," but is it limited to that? Think before you answer. In fact, look down at verse 15:

"All things that the Father has are Mine; therefore I said, that
He takes of Mine, and will disclose it to you."
John 16:15

If one of the Spirit's tasks is to guide us into and disclose the truth, who says that means only the truth of Scripture? Why couldn't it include the truth of His will? Or the truth about another person? Or the truth regarding both sides of a tough decision? Why couldn't those things be a part of "what is to come," which He promised "to disclose" to you and me?

I am devoting chapter 7 to the inner promptings of the Spirit, so there is no need for me to take a lot of time now to develop these thoughts. But it may be helpful to spend a few minutes pondering the questions I just asked.

Think about times in your own past when the Spirit guided you or disclosed something to you. It might have occurred when you were stuck in a passage of Scripture. You needed to understand what it meant, but nothing came clear. And then, to your surprise, in a relatively brief period of time everything opened up. I cannot number the times that has happened to me.

And haven't you struggled with a decision? The more you wrestled, the greater the struggle. In the beginning you felt as if you were standing in a thick, dark cloud. Then, gradually, the fog lifted and you could see your way through. I am suggesting that such can be traced to the Spirit's work of revealing.

Interestingly, Jesus said, "He will not speak on His own initiative, but whatever He hears, He will speak." I find that a curious remark. Not "whatever He reads," as if He were looking over our shoulder into the pages of the Bible, but "whatever He hears." From whom does He "hear" the things He reveals? I believe the ultimate source must be God the Father. After all, it is His plan that is being worked out.

I can think of several surprising moments when I have been the recipient of the Spirit's disclosures.

- Biblical insights I would otherwise have missed.

- A sudden awareness of God's will or the presence of danger or a sense of peace in the midst of chaos.

- A surge of bold confidence in a setting where there would otherwise have been fear and hesitation.

- A quiet, calm awareness that I was not alone, even though no one else was actually with me.

- The undeniable, surrounding awareness of evil . . . even the dark sinister presence of demonic forces.

In each case I was made aware of "the truth," which the Spirit disclosed to me. It was either there at the moment or it soon (sometimes later) was revealed to me.

While I was counseling with a troubled individual recently, the person became exceedingly anxious. Tears flowed. Feelings of panic seized him and he shook uncontrollably. It was an extremely emotional moment for him as his wife sat near him, feeling so helpless. Then, seemingly out of nowhere, I got a flash of insight, sparked by something she said. It tied in beautifully with a scriptural principle I had spoken on several days earlier. The wife's comment, coupled with the biblical principle, plus a thought that came to me as the three of us sat together, led me to say a sentence or two, nothing more. The result was a total surprise.

The man suddenly paused and stared into my eyes. He blinked several times without saying a word. I could tell he was processing the information. He wiped the tears from his face, shook his head a time or two, and said, "That's it. That is exactly what I needed to hear, but I couldn't—I needed to figure it out." He stood up, gave me a firm handshake, and left with his arm around his smiling wife.

What happened? I am convinced the Spirit who surprises guided us into that moment of truth and with surgical precision revealed the statement that needed to be said and heard.

Some Examples of the Spirit's Inner Workings

What Jesus taught before He went to the cross and ultimately left the earth, the apostle Paul addresses in a little more detail in his letter to the Corinthians. That explains why we have some examples in 1 Corinthians 2 of the Spirit's inner workings.

The more I look into these things, the more fascinated I am by them. The more I dig below the surface, the more I am beginning to see how much I have missed before in my study of the Scriptures. So much of what He does is so surprising that we usually think of it only as coincidence. Because we cannot see the Spirit of God, we tend to overlook His presence in our midst in general and in our individual lives in particular.

Demonstrating God's Unique Power

In his letter to the Corinthians, the apostle Paul looks back on his early days in Corinth when he was just founding the church, and he calls to mind his ministry when he was among them. I find it significant that the very first thing he puts his finger on is the demonstration of God's unique power as he gives his own testimony about the Corinthian ministry.

> And when I came to you, brethren, I did not come with superiority of speech or of wisdom, proclaiming to you the testimony of God.
>
> 1 Corinthians 2:1

He states first what he did *not* do. He did not come strutting a self-serving, fleshly motivated superiority of speech or displaying his wisdom.

Was he a brilliant man? You know he was brilliant. He had studied under Gamaliel and other exceptional mentors. And famous? Saul of Tarsus was surely a household name among century-one Jews. He was the up-and-coming Sanhedrinist. He was a Pharisee of Pharisees. He was the arch persecutor of the church.

He was a man with advanced degrees and relentless passion. It is not an overstatement to say he was second to none.

And then—*surprise!* The Spirit of God entered his life at his conversion, and the apostle Paul went through a transformation that changed his whole direction in life. His entire approach, his entire philosophy of life, was altered. So transforming was the change that when he came to this "ancient entertainment center," Corinth of Greece, to serve the Lord among people who looked for impressive eloquence and fleshly demonstrations of human wisdom, he deliberately refused to perform for their satisfaction. Paul had no interest in being a "showstopper."

Well, what *did* he do?

> For I determined to know nothing among you except Jesus Christ, and Him crucified. And I was with you in weakness and in fear and in much trembling.
>
> 1 Corinthians 2:2–3

Go back and ponder his self-description: "weakness . . . fear . . . trembling." Now, if I were to ask you to describe Paul, I doubt that you would use any one of those three words. Because when we think of Paul, we think of a man of enormous strength and capability, a man who had the ability to speak on any subject with hardly a misplaced word. In fact, Apollos was the eloquent one, not Paul, who came with apparent weakness, in a spirit of fear and also much trembling.

By the way, Paul's honesty is a good reminder for you and me when we find ourselves in places where we are intimidated, where we feel fearful and very weak. Surprisingly, that is when the Spirit of God does His best work. For when you and I are weak, God shows His strength.

Paul learned that, as he writes in 2 Corinthians 12. The Lord showed him that when he was weak and unable, incapable and inadequate, God took up the slack. The ministry of the Spirit of God came in like a flood and made those occasions the most powerful and profound of his life and ministry in Corinth.

How could he have been strong in his weakness, powerful in his fears, and effective in his trembling? The answer is in verses 4 and 5.

> And my message and my preaching were not in persuasive words of wisdom, but in demonstration of the Spirit and of power, that your faith should not rest on the wisdom of men, but on the power of God.
>
> 1 Corinthians 2:4–5

There's that word again—*power,* from the Greek term *dunamis.* It keeps resurfacing in our study of the Spirit—a dynamic invariably linked to the Holy Spirit.

When the Corinthian believers left the meetings where they had come to be ministered to by Paul, they left talking about the Lord, not the one who had ministered. And that pleased Paul immensely. Why? Because he had received *dunamis* from the Helper! The Helper empowered the man's message, ignited his leadership, and shaped his inimitable style. As a result, the awesome presence of God was felt.

Don't be afraid either of those words or of that reality. Don't resist it because it seems "too emotional." There are occasions where the presence of God is so obvious that it is like electricity upon the gathering. I have been in certain meetings when everyone in attendance was able to sense the dynamic power of the Spirit of God.

The most recent experience I had like this occurred while I was ministering earlier this year in Brisbane, Australia. Several of our leadership team from my radio ministry, "Insight for Living," had been invited to a church on the east coast of "the land down under." We weren't in the meeting ten minutes before we realized how obviously present the Spirit of God was. The music was full of joyful, meaningful praise. There were spontaneous occasions that added to the refreshing delight of the evening. I sensed unusual freedom as I spoke and as people listened and responded. I did not know the folks who were there, and they had never seen me before. Prior to that occasion I had only been to Australia once, so culturally I was a novice. But the bond that formed between us was instant and genuine. I loved it!

As our leadership team left, we agreed: This was clearly the work of the Spirit. Later, as we tried to describe to others the significance of that time, we could not do it. Furthermore, I have discovered that such Spirit-empowered occasions cannot be duplicated. It isn't like a stage play, where one outstanding performance after another can be repeated. The work of God's Spirit is absolutely unique.

Paul's experience among the Corinthians, by his own testimony, was clearly a demonstration of the work of the Spirit. Not unlike our Brisbane meeting, God was in it from start to finish.

Searching God's Hidden Wisdom

Having introduced the "demonstration of the Spirit," Paul digs even deeper as he writes about His "searching" work. Read the following words slowly and carefully:

> Yet we do speak wisdom among those who are mature; a wisdom, however, not of this age, nor of the rulers of this age, who are passing away; but we speak God's wisdom in a mystery, the hidden wisdom, which God predestined before the ages to our glory; the wisdom which none of the rulers of this age has understood; for if they had understood it, they would not have crucified the Lord of glory; but just as it is written,
>
> "THINGS WHICH EYE HAS NOT SEEN AND
>   EAR HAS NOT HEARD,
> AND WHICH HAVE NOT ENTERED THE
>   HEART OF MAN,
> ALL THAT GOD HAS PREPARED FOR THOSE
>   WHO LOVE HIM."
>
> 1 Corinthians 2:6–9

The apostle returns to Isaiah's words and paraphrases them, probably drawing from the Septuagint, which was the Bible of Paul's day.

We are unable, he says, in and of ourselves, to sit down and figure out the "wisdom of God"—regardless of how much intelligence one may have or how many advanced degrees one has earned. God's wisdom is not discovered from such human sources. The human mind, all on its own, cannot plumb the depths of God's truths. You and I are dependent upon Another to know them. Those truths must come from the Godhead. And the One appointed to that specific task? The Holy Spirit, who lives within every child of God. He resides within us, not to be dormant and passive, but actively engaged in revealing God's hidden wisdom. Neither can we glean such wisdom from one another. Deep, divine wisdom must come from God as we allow ourselves to fly closer to the flame.

Let's go further:

> For to us God revealed them through the Spirit; for the Spirit
> searches all things, even the depths of God.
> 1 Corinthians 2:10

Another surprise! The Spirit of God is the One who gleans truth from within the Godhead and then reveals this wisdom to individuals like you and me. Thanks to the Holy Spirit, such deep truths are deposited into our minds. Without the Helper's supernatural assistance, we're sunk! He must reveal, or we don't receive.

I sometimes think of the Holy Spirit as a deep-sea diver who goes to the depths searching for treasures. The diver drops off the side of the boat. As the bubbles rise to the water's surface, he drops deeper, deeper, deeper . . . probing through all the mysteries of the deep that the human eye cannot see from above. Finally he surfaces again, bringing with him treasures from some sunken vessel. Sometimes the treasures are so precious they are priceless. Without the diver, however, they would remain hidden forever.

The Spirit of God, in the same manner, searches the deepest realms of the wisdom of God to lift out truths we need to know and understand. He not only digs them up, He is able to bring them to our attention. What a magnificently important work!

> Oh, the depth of the riches both of the wisdom and knowledge of God! How unsearchable are His judgments and unfathomable His ways! FOR WHO HAS KNOWN THE MIND OF THE LORD, OR WHO BECAME HIS COUNSELOR? OR WHO HAS FIRST GIVEN TO HIM THAT IT MIGHT BE PAID BACK TO HIM AGAIN? For from Him and through Him and to Him are all things. To Him be the glory forever. Amen.
>
> Romans 11:33–36

Theology has been called "the queen of the sciences." Before it, all other earthly truths must bow. Only those who have a grasp of the wisdom and the magnificent, profound, unfathomable plan of God can fit truth into its proper place in whatever era they may live. A true education occurs when theology is given its proper priority. Our forefathers knew that. That is why, when the earliest universities were founded, it was for the purpose of establishing a literate and learned ministry, so that the people might continue to keep the wisdom of God in focus with the needs of human beings.

Revealing God's Deep Thoughts

In the Corinthian letter, Paul refers to the same "depth of God" that he mentioned in Romans 11.

> For who among men knows the thoughts of a man except the spirit of the man, which is in him? Even so the thoughts of God no one knows except the Spirit of God.
>
> 1 Corinthians 2:11

If I could look deeply into your eyes and study you for several hours, I would still be unable to know what was going on in your mind. I would also be unable to tell what was in your spirit. Yet you and I are aware of what is going on in our own minds, aren't we?

Within the mind of God there is this vast, unfathomable treasure house of truth called "wisdom." Obviously it is all known by the living God. And the Spirit of God, being deity Himself, knows all of that mysterious, hidden, magnificent wisdom. It comprises a body of truth that is essential for living; in fact, sometimes it is essential for surviving the times in which we live. Now the "clincher" is—

> Now we have received, not the spirit of the world, but the Spirit who is from God, that we might know the things freely given to us by God.
>
> 1 Corinthians 2:12

Is that marvelous or what? At the moment of salvation, you and I were given the Spirit of God. We were identified with the body of Christ. We were made a part of the family. Included in that "original package" was the profound workings of the Holy Spirit within our being. As He came to live within us, He was fully equipped to reveal God's wisdom, having searched the deep things of God. And what a vital body of truth it is!

When we are facing an impasse, the Spirit of God is there to assist us through it. When we are experiencing grief and loss, the Spirit of God is there to give wisdom and insight in the crucible of our pain. When we encounter the unknown, the Spirit of God is there to keep us from being intimidated. He lives within us to reveal, to teach, to direct. And how often those things that come from Him are total surprises—far beyond human thoughts. As Isaiah wrote, the thoughts that come from God are "high above the earth" and totally different from mere human knowledge.

Let me go one step further and say that this may very well explain how you and I can have inner confidence and assurance regarding certain matters when others don't. Haven't you had that happen? You have pored over something in prayer, waited on God, searched His truths in the Scriptures, and then come to a settled conviction: "This is what I ought to do." Or perhaps, "This is what I ought not to do." Others don't agree with you. Others around you cannot see the logic of it. Yet it is as though you are "bound in the Spirit" to carry out your conviction because you know it is what God would have you do. It may seem surprising to some and stupid to others, but you know it's what you must do. The longer I live, the more I believe that that kind of wisdom, conviction, and knowledge is the work of the Spirit.

I want to show you an example. A scene very similar to the one I just described actually happened among the leaders in Ephesus as Paul was saying good-bye. They were about to put their arms around each other and bid farewell for the last time. But just before they did, Paul told them:

> "And now, behold, bound in spirit, I am on my way to Jerusalem, not knowing what will happen to me there, except that the Holy Spirit solemnly testifies to me in every city, saying that bonds and afflictions await me. But I do not consider my life of any account as dear to myself, in order that I may finish my course, and the ministry which I received from the Lord Jesus, to testify solemnly of the gospel of the grace of God."
>
> Acts 20:22–24

Look at that! The Holy Spirit is literally *testifying* to Paul. And what is He saying? He is saying that "in every city bonds and afflictions" will occur. We shall look at this scene in much greater detail later, but for now try to imagine Paul's confidence, which grew out of the Spirit's "inner voice."

The Spirit does not always lead us into places of comfort. Sometimes it is God's surprising plan to lead us into a difficult place to serve as His representative. Paul's experience was just that. He was saying, in effect, "I'm going to Jerusalem, and I know before I get there that trouble awaits." And that is exactly what happened. If you study the rest of the story, you will see a man dependent on God for survival.

The Spirit revealed much of what awaited Paul, testifying that "bonds and afflictions" were on the horizon of his future. Well, if he knew this ahead of time, some may ask, why would he go on such a threatening mission? Because he was God's servant. Obedience out of self-sacrificial trust was his only option.

> "But I do not consider my life of any account as dear to myself, in order that I may finish my course, and the ministry which I received from the Lord Jesus, to testify solemnly of the gospel of the grace of God."
>
> Acts 20:24

That is what I call having the long view of life. If we were only looking at today, we would be very cautious, very protective of ourselves. But we must look at life in light of eternity. We are a part of the plan. Like Paul, our desire must be to finish the course, strong in faith.

Paul could say: "I'm on my way to Jerusalem. And I know that difficulties await me, because through the Spirit, I have been given this insight. God made it clear to me." Some today would be tempted to call this a premonition. I would not use that word to describe the Spirit's work within us. Rather, this is the preliminary prompting of the Holy Spirit within us. I freely confess that it is difficult to pin it down. It's hard to describe it in exact terms. It is like nailing a poached egg to a tree. You can't get everything to stick. Certainly, in this case, it was the surprising work of the Spirit in Paul's life.

Teaching God's Profound Insights

And so it is the Spirit of God who takes the things of God and communicates them to His own. How? Read Paul's comment very carefully:

. . . which things we also speak, not in words taught by human wisdom, but in those taught by the Spirit, combining spiritual thoughts with spiritual words.

1 Corinthians 2:13

By the Spirit's "combining spiritual thoughts with spiritual words," we are led into new and unexpected territory. We have a growing confidence in His providing all the strength we'll need to face whatever lies ahead. Because . . .

- We have a "Helper" who has been "called alongside."
- In place of weakness, He brings power.
- In place of ignorance, He brings knowledge.
- In place of human knowledge, He brings divine wisdom and profound insights from the depths of God's plan.
- As we grasp these depths, combining spiritual thoughts and words, we gain confidence in His will.
- And even though it may be surprising, when God is in it, there is only one option: *obedience.*

Which brings us back to where this chapter started: my surprising awareness that I should stop resisting and respond in the affirmative to the call to become the next president of Dallas Theological Seminary.

Somehow, in His perfect plan, this is His will for me. And because that is true, I have only one option. It is obedience.

But I am *still* surprised.

6

Draw Me Nearer . . . Nearer

$\mathcal{A}$RE YOU PLEASED WITH your Christian walk? By that I mean, are you absolutely, unequivocally, and unconditionally satisfied with the level of your relationship with Christ . . . with the power of God's presence in your life? Or do you, in unguarded moments, entertain thoughts like:

I wonder if there may be more?

I wonder if my prayer life could be more passionate, more dynamic, more confident?

Is the Lord really first in my thinking?

When I get sick, why do I first think of calling my doctor instead of calling on my God?

Why, when I have a serious financial need, do I first think of some bank I could go to for a loan rather than the courts of heaven for divine assistance?

Well, if those sorts of thoughts trouble you, you are not alone.

Let me read you a few excerpts from a letter I received from a friend of mine whom I greatly respect. He is a Christian businessman, works for a Christian organization, has a fine Christian wife and family. He is an Evangelical, a conservative, but he is not what some would call a "charismatic" Christian. I say all that not to typecast him, but to help you understand where he is coming from.

In the section of his letter he calls "scatter-shooting," he writes:

There's a yearning in the evangelical world for a greater sense of intimacy with God. I believe we have had too much head and not enough heart.

People are intrigued now with the Holy Spirit. Like the proverbial moth and flame, they don't know how close they can fly without burning their wings. They are attracted to the flame for some unexplainable reason; still, they are frightened by the Holy Spirit.

There is a fear among us Evangelicals that we have missed out on something spiritually. The abundant life we've sought is not altogether fulfilling. There is a craving for spiritual intimacy with God that is seldom, if ever, satisfied. Could it be that what is really missing—the thing that would give us an appetite for daily prayer and Bible study and personal dynamic—is the empowering of a more profound measure of the Holy Spirit? Don't we need to let the Holy Spirit out of the closet?

Evangelicals may have believed the spiritual world is flat; that if they sail too close to the edge of the Christian experience, they'll fall off the edge into emotional oblivion. So we've run away from all but the most intellectualized expressions of the Spirit, as though He were some kind of sea monster.

Evangelicals are "reasoned believers," almost too logical, yet we've always suspected that too much emotion has been let out of our Christian experience. Many of us yearn for spiritual passion, which has become only a flicker of light, to be turned up several notches. Somebody with evangelical credibility needs to tell us that it's okay to get closer to the flame. [He then challenges me to do that.]

Maybe God still works miracles—at least in some measure. If not, then why do we pray for God's help when we are sick or diseased? Are our prayers for God's intervention merely psychological games we play on ourselves, knowing that God no longer acts decisively (much less miraculously) in our world today? Evangelicals are secretly concerned that we have become "deists" who think God's last acts were a few miracles after the Resurrection. Since about A.D. 70, has God gone off into the back room, leaving blind spiritual and physical laws in control? Isn't there an option besides deism and Oral Roberts? Can we free God to work pro-actively in His world?

Let's face it, Chuck, the Charismatics scare us. We are secretly relieved when fringe nuts like [he names several well-known extremists] have their sordid laundry aired out in the press. The truth is that mainstream Charismatics are also embarrassed by such extremists. Let's don't throw the baby out with the bath water.

How would a new, unintimidated theology of the Holy Spirit change our experiences in worship, in prayer, in witness, in spiritual confidence? Some of us need a revolution, Chuck.

Isn't it about time Evangelicals revisited the doctrine of the Holy Spirit without concern that it will sound too charismatic? Shouldn't we leave God more room to work directly in our lives today? E.T. has had a deeper, more positive personal impact on the lives of some people than the Holy Spirit.

After you've had a chance to review this letter, I'd love to visit with you by phone. I may be so far off-base that it scares you to death. If so, I'll understand.[1]

I love that man. I love his courage. I love his probing mind, his honesty, his creativity. I am especially impressed that he isn't afraid to put his finger on a nerve and push a little harder. Even if it makes some of us uncomfortable and uneasy, at least it makes us think!

The tragedy is that some have stopped thinking altogether. For many in the conservative evangelical ranks the quest is over. There is nothing more to discover, no new territory to examine, nothing else to experience. As the old saying goes, they are "saved, sanctified, galvanized, and petrified." That troubles me most of all.

Now on behalf of many of us, let me make an open and unguarded confession: There are times you and I desire more fulfilling expressions of faith. There are times we wish for more evidences of the dynamic of the Spirit of God in our lives. But fear restrains us! Fear of being misunderstood by our brothers and sisters in the faith . . . fear of being mislabeled . . . fear of going off the emotional deep end and getting weird . . . fear of getting away from Scripture and slipping into error. We are afraid of wading too far out into the doctrinal waters, getting way over our heads, then not being able to swim back to shore.

Now I can just hear some of you saying, "Swindoll is losing it. Next he'll be going to Tibet to meditate on top of some mountain." Don't bet on it.

Please, be assured, I have never in my life been more committed to the Scriptures. I was born in 1934, so I'm no spring chicken . . . yet at this age, I can honestly say that I love Christ more deeply and believe His Word more firmly than ever in my life. Virtually every day of my life I am digging into the treasures of the Word of God. So let me put your mind at ease. I am probably more theologically orthodox than I've ever been in my life. But that does not mean I have stopped learning. I am still thinking, and I am still dissatisfied with the status quo.

The fact of the matter is, I simply am not convinced that our understanding and appropriation of the Holy Spirit is all it can be or all it should be. While I don't think we need "more of God" (an impossibility, since we have all of Him!), I do think we need to act upon all that we have. I don't believe we need to pray for some new thing to come upon us, but I do believe we need to appropriate in much greater measure what is already within us.

It's like the brain. During our entire lives, we use maybe one-tenth or less of it—one tiny portion of it—and the rest of it just lies there like a gray glob, learning nothing new, just marking time. I cannot believe that is God's desire for His people when it comes to the spiritual resources He has given us.

As I have already written, I think the Spirit of God, who resides inside every believer, is ready to take charge and instill within us not only a dynamic but also a quiet confidence in life. Yet most sort of stumble along from day to day virtually unaware of or unconcerned about the vast provisions that are ours to claim.

My prayer is that we remain open and teachable—like my friend—and that our God may lead us and reveal fresh truths from His Word, including blowing some of the dust off old truths and bringing them back to life. I hope the pages of this book will clear the debris from some great truths that await our appropriation.

I want to spend the rest of my years challenging people to go to the very edge of their faith . . . to risk new thoughts . . . ponder new ideas . . . enter into new experiences without fear. The truth is, we have pulled too far back from some of the best things the Lord has for us.

A Closer Examination That Enlightens Us

If we are going to fly a lot closer to the sacred flame, we need to relearn and hopefully rediscover by closer examination what He has said in His Book. For example, let's return to Ephesians 5. Here we find a list of don'ts.

- Ephesians 5:3. *Don't be immoral, impure, or greedy.*

    But do not let immorality or any impurity or greed even be named among you, as is proper among saints.

- Ephesians 5:4. *Don't lose control of your tongue.*

    . . . and there must be no filthiness and silly talk, or coarse jesting, which are not fitting, but rather giving of thanks.

- Ephesians 5:6. *Don't be deceived.*

    Let no one deceive you with empty words, for because of these things the wrath of God comes upon the sons of disobedience.

- Ephesians 5:11. *Don't participate in evil deeds . . . deeds of darkness.*

    And do not participate in the unfruitful deeds of darkness, but instead even expose them.

- Ephesians 5:15. *Don't be unwise.*

    Therefore be careful how you walk, not as unwise men, but as wise.

- Ephesians 5:17. *Don't be foolish.*

  So then do not be foolish, but understand what the will of the Lord is.

- Ephesians 5:18. *Don't get drunk.*

  And do not get drunk with wine, for that is dissipation, but be filled with the Spirit.

All these don'ts tell me that God cares more about the details of our personal lives than most folks would ever believe. He names these things, calling them to our attention, because they will hurt us if we tolerate and/or traffic in them.

He then brings everything to a climax as He offers one grand, positive command. After "Don't, don't, don't, don't, don't, don't, don't," He says, "Do" (at least that's the implied directive).

- Ephesians 5:18 ". . . *but be filled with the Spirit.*"

In place of all these things that the world will try to tell you are emotionally and physically stimulating, come back to the person of the intimate Spirit and let Him fill your life.

When the Lord delivered your salvation, His Spirit came within you as part of the package deal, remember? The Spirit was in the initial "gift package." Without your even knowing it, the Spirit of God took up permanent residence within you. And when He entered your life, He brought with Him—for you—the full capacity of His power. Without Christ, you and I were like a vast, empty reservoir awaiting the coming of a downpour. As salvation became a reality, this emptiness became full to the point of running over. The Spirit of God has filled our internal capacity with power and dynamic.

Now in light of that, allow Him to take full control! That is the command. Instead of being filled with alcohol, instead of being filled with drugs, instead of being filled with filthy talk, instead of being filled with immorality, be filled with the dynamic Spirit of God. Like the wind that fills the sails, allow His power to propel your life.

Is He filling you like that? Have you responded to God's strong command?

Can you think of a time in your life when you really could say, "I remember being so filled with the thoughts of God and the power of God that I felt invincible in the midst of my trials"? That is what can happen. More importantly, that's what God wants for us. We can truly and actually be "filled" with His dynamic power.

A wonderful example of this is recorded in Acts 6, where it tells how the apostles were engaged in leading the early church. And wouldn't you know it? A complaint arose because some of the people in the church didn't have enough food. The problem was exacerbated by the fact that some were being helped while others were being overlooked. At the heart of the problem was preferential treatment. While the local Jews were being cared for, the Hellenistic Jews were being ignored.

> Now at this time while the disciples were increasing in number, a complaint arose on the part of the Hellenistic Jews against the native Hebrews, because their widows were being overlooked in the daily serving of food. And the twelve summoned the congregation of the disciples and said, "It is not desirable for us to neglect the word of God in order to serve tables."
>
> Acts 6:1–2

Perhaps we could call this one of the earliest church business meetings! There may have been hundreds present, maybe thousands. After everyone had gathered, the apostles told them that something had to be done. Somebody needed to help in the daily serving of food to the needy.

> "But select from among you, brethren, seven men of good reputation, full of the Spirit and of wisdom, whom we may put in charge of this task. But we will devote ourselves to prayer, and to the ministry of the word."
>
> Acts 6:3–4

Isn't that an interesting list of qualifications for service? From among them (implying that not everyone would meet the qualifications), they were to choose seven men of "good reputation," full of "wisdom," and "full of the Spirit." Here in the early church, the leaders—the apostles—were saying they wanted Spirit-filled men to carry out this role of service.

And the others agreed with their assessment, for "the statement found approval with the whole congregation" (6:5).

As a result, "they chose Stephen," who is identified as "a man full of faith and of the Holy Spirit." Stephen was a man in whom the intimate Spirit was carrying out His dynamic work. His sail was full of the blessed wind of the Spirit. The flame of God had set his spirit ablaze. He was moving through life with the hand of God upon him. He was walking in the light, abiding in the vine.

Shortly after being selected, Stephen was cornered by:

> . . . some men from what was called the Synagogue of the Freedmen, including both Cyrenians and Alexandrians, and some from Cilicia and Asia.
>
> Acts 6:9

These men "rose up and argued with Stephen." Could Stephen hold his own before a threatening crowd like that? You better believe it! We read that his antagonists:

> were unable to cope with the wisdom and the Spirit with which he was speaking.
>
> Acts 6:10

His critics lacked sufficient strength to take a stand against him. Literally, they were unable to *withstand*. With Stephen's inner being filled to capacity with the igniting presence of the Spirit, they didn't stand a chance. Stephen must have been wired!

A. T. Robertson suggests that, "Stephen was like a battery charged and in action."[2] That doesn't mean he ran roughshod over people. It means that under the dominant control of the Spirit, he was unintimidated by and invincible before his critics.

Bold as a lion, confident in God, under the full control of the Spirit of God, he moved through the waters of resistance without getting off course. They were unable to hold him back. The Spirit's filling was obvious to all.

Make no mistake, they hated him because of that. The opposition party grew increasingly more hostile, until their anger and their hatred turned to murder.

> Then they secretly induced men to say, "We have heard him speak blasphemous words against Moses and against God." And they stirred up the people, the elders and the scribes, and they came upon him and dragged him away, and brought him before the Council. And they put forward false witnesses who said, "This man incessantly speaks against this holy place, and the Law; for we have heard him say that this Nazarene, Jesus, will destroy this place and alter the customs which Moses handed down to us." And fixing their gaze on him, all who were sitting in the Council saw his face like the face of an angel.
>
> Acts 6:11–15

What does that mean? Well, having never seen an angel, it is difficult to say. I would suspect Stephen glowed. Almost without exception, where there are evidences of the presence of heaven upon earth there is an aura—like a glowing, shining light. In this case, I believe it was visible, which explains why they said he had the "face of an angel."

In spite of the mounting pressure Stephen was facing, he delivered a sermon, among the best I have ever read. Standing before the angry group of people—their arms folded, their frowns deep, their jaws set, and their minds fixed on stoning the preacher—Stephen preached. (Sounds like some church situations today!)

Ever spoken to a hostile crowd? Probably never this hostile. I remember preaching Christ from free-speech platforms in the 1960s. Talk about exciting! Places like the University of Oklahoma in Norman . . . the University of California at Berkeley.

What stretching, exciting experiences! You had to be Spirit-filled or you could never have withstood their verbal attacks. Some even threw things at us. But that was like saying "Sic 'em" to a hungry Rottweiler. Churchill's words had new meaning: "Few things in life are more exhilarating than being shot at without result."

In times like that, God's Spirit gives unintimidated confidence. That's precisely what Stephen had. Remember, the man was filled with God's Spirit. He was the personification of cool, calm courage.

What happened? Hold on tight. The scene gets ugly.

> Now when they heard this, they were cut to the quick, and they began gnashing their teeth at him.
>
> Acts 7:54

They were livid!

> But being full of the Holy Spirit, he gazed intently into heaven and saw the glory of God, and Jesus standing at the right hand of God.
>
> Acts 7:55

"But being full of the Holy Spirit . . . "—why would the writer suddenly insert that comment? Because that was the unseen source of Stephen's strength. That was the reason behind his invincibility and perseverance. I am confident that his voice didn't even tremble.

Incredible. With death's hot breath blowing against the back of his neck, Stephen literally saw that ageless, penetrating light of God's glory pouring out of heaven. Full of the Spirit, he saw what no other eyes could see. He testified,

> "Behold, I see the heavens opened up and the Son of Man standing at the right hand of God."
>
> Acts 7:56

Not only did he see the glory of God, he saw Jesus standing at the right hand of God. (By the way, remember when Christ ascended? The Scriptures state that at that time our Lord was *seated* at the right hand of the throne of God. But Stephen saw Jesus standing up. I wonder . . . maybe He stands up for certain individuals when they die. Perhaps, with nail-scarred hands outstretched, He was saying, "Come on home, sweet Stephen. Come on home, dear servant of Mine. Enough of that.")

On the basis of this account, I wonder if those filled with the Spirit at certain moments of desperate crisis in their lives are enabled to witness things no one else can see?

Just wondering . . .

> But they cried out with a loud voice, and covered their ears, and they rushed upon him with one impulse. And when they had driven him out of the city, they began stoning him, and the witnesses laid aside their robes at the feet of a young man named Saul. And they went on stoning Stephen as he called upon the Lord and said, "Lord Jesus, receive my spirit!" And falling on his knees, he cried out with a loud voice, "Lord, do not hold this sin against them!" And having said this, he fell asleep.
>
> Acts 7:57–60

Somehow God gave Stephen the supernatural ability to deliver a message in the mist of insuperable odds. Even at that incredible moment, he offers words of praise to God and words of forgiveness to his murderers. Is that kind of "overcoming" part of the filling of the Spirit? It was for Stephen. Why shouldn't it be for us?

Is that the kind of walk with Christ you have? Is that the dynamic that is characterizing your life these days? If so, you are rare, I can assure you. If not, why not? If that is possible, then why aren't there similar manifestations in our circles today?

Just asking . . .

Questions and Observations That Intrigue Us

It was almost as if his being filled with the Spirit provided Stephen with some kind of special readiness for battle. Could this have been some kind of "anointing"?

Again, I'm just asking . . .

Let's begin our probe into the "anointing" of the Spirit by reviewing a couple of things we learned earlier. Do you recall why we have received the Spirit? First Corinthians 2 explains:

> Now we have received, not the spirit of the world, but the Spirit who is from God, that we might know the things freely given to us from God, which things we also speak, not in words taught by human wisdom, but in those taught by the Spirit, combining spiritual *thoughts* with spiritual *words*.
>
> 2 Corinthians 2:12–13

First, we received "the Spirit who is from God" that we might "speak" the thoughts given to us by God ("combining spiritual *thoughts* with spiritual *words*").

> But a natural man does not accept the things of the Spirit of God; for they are foolishness to him, and he cannot understand them, because they are spiritually appraised. But he who is spiritual appraises all things, yet he himself is appraised by no man.
>
> 2 Corinthians 2:14–15

And second, we received the Spirit that we might "appraise all things."

Appraise means "to sift, to discern." Is that part of the filling? No doubt. By being filled with the Spirit, we are given a discernment that filters incidentals from essentials, truth from error. In other words, Christians are provided with an inner filtering system.

Now we are ready for 1 John 2, which speaks of the "anointing" from God. This is a letter clearly written to believers, whom John affectionately calls "little children."

> But you have an anointing from the Holy One, and you all
> know.
>
> 1 John 2:20

Some translations of the Bible put the "all" at the end of the sentence: "And you know all," which makes it sound like when you have an anointing, you have all knowledge. I think, rather, that the original text suggests that "all" is the subject—"you all know." So? So it's for everyone. "Little children, you have an anointing, and all of you, therefore, have a knowledge." There is something from God that links anointing with knowing.

> And as for you, the anointing which you received from Him
> abides in you, and you have no need for any one to teach you;
> but as His anointing teaches you about all things, and is true
> and is not a lie, and just as it has taught you, you abide in
> Him.
>
> 1 John 2:27

This particular usage of *anointing* is found only three times in the New Testament, and all three are in this chapter of 1 John. The term comes from the Greek word *chrisma*. In ancient days, chrisma was an ointment, like a thick oil. Kings were anointed with chrisma, as were priests when they were inducted into the sacred office.

On the basis of that, I suggest that this "anointing" happens once, which explains John's comment, "You have an anointing." Also, John says that it "abides in you." So it is permanent; this "anointing" won't leave. Each believer has it. It happens once. It is permanent. And it "teaches you about all things."

The original word here is *oida*, which means knowledge, but not *experiential* knowledge.

Electricity is in all our homes; we're aware of it. That's *oida* knowledge. We know it theoretically, intellectually. If I get a paper clip and go to an electrical outlet in my home and stick that little piece of metal in the slot, suddenly I *experience* electricity! That's *ginosko* knowledge.

My point here is that John uses *oida*, not *ginosko*. Which tells us that there is something about the Holy Spirit's presence that provides you and me with an innate knowledge, an inner awareness. Such knowledge is included in the anointing.

In other words, you and I have a sixth sense. It is something that the worldling does not have, because he doesn't have the Spirit. When you have Christ, you have the Spirit. And when you have the Spirit, you have the anointing. You know something that cannot be taught and cannot be learned. You have a discernment, a built-in awareness, an inner compass, if you will.

Would this anointing explain what we commonly call intuition? I don't know, but I do think it's in that family. Are we giving credit to intuition that really belongs to the Holy Spirit? I cannot say for sure, but perhaps we are.

Here's another intriguing question: If we are full of the Spirit, can we envision things others cannot? Again, I'm not affirming it, I'm only asking. Since Stephen was able to do so, can any believer? Since the Spirit searches all things, could He give us insight and on-the-spot discernment that transcend human ability, academic learning, and personal training? He's God; why couldn't He?

And if that is true, wouldn't those who oppose us find themselves unable to stand against us . . . unable to "withstand"? I lean toward saying yes. It's what we might call a "supernatural sense of invincibility." And at times I have experienced it, that underlying sense of absolute confidence. Perhaps you have as well. In those moments of unusual courage—without any credit to myself—I am not afraid to stand absolutely alone.

Could that inner confidence be part of the anointing?

A Few Words of Warning

I hope all this won't get kicked sideways in your mind and twist up some awfully good theology. To keep that from happening, let me caution you with a few words of warning.

Balance is always preferred to extremes. So as I previously reminded you: *Keep your balance in all things.* A scriptural word for it is *moderation.* Stay reasonable, Christian friend. Don't go home and start praying for some middle-of-the-night visions; that's not biblical. Keep a level head. Don't get weird.

Don't start looking for the face of Jesus in an enchilada. Or try to convince me that some cloud formation represents the Last Supper. Don't start setting dates for Jesus' return. Don't play with snakes and scorpions. Don't sacrifice your solid biblical roots and orthodox theology on the altar of bizarre experiences. Don't start attending meetings where legs are lengthened and teeth are filled. That kind of sideshow stuff may draw a crowd, but it is not the anointing.

The anointing is a knowledge. You know something. You discern something. It is an inner awareness. It is a surge of strengthening assurance. And never forget it always exalts the Lord and gives all glory to God.

Let me also add: *Stay with the Scriptures.* While our individual experiences may vary somewhat as the Lord uses each of us in unique ways, we must never—and I mean never—get too far from the revealed and reliable Word of God. If you do, you will begin to use your experience as a basis for your beliefs, and the Scriptures will diminish in importance as you make more and more room for more strange experiences.

I have pastor friends who have done just that. And today when I talk with them, I find that they no longer believe that the Bible is God's *final* Word. They are now convinced that He is still revealing inspired truth. My reaction? Whoa! If that's true, then how do I know where His Word starts and their vivid imagination stops . . . and how much of it can I trust? No matter how persuasive the preacher, you and I need God's inspired Word, not additional revelations of "truth." When *that* happens, we are hopelessly awash.

One theologian has sounded a very wise warning:

> The issue of Biblical inspiration and authority lies close
> to the heart of Christian theology. It is a continental divide

running through the center of its landscape. Where we stand on the divine integrity of Scripture will determine the nature and content of the gospel we proclaim to the world. . . .

The distinctive mark of theology in our day is its dreadful ambiguity. Something needs to be done to check the pretended autonomy of this unbiblical thought. The chaos of American theology today can be traced back to its roots in the rejection of Biblical infallibility. For Christian theology rests upon the truth claim implicit in the doctrine of inspiration. Scripture is the principium of theology. Only because the Bible embodies objectively true communication about the nature of God, the condition of man, and the provision of His salvation, is it possible to begin the theological task. The question of inspiration is then not the plaything of the theological specialist; it is the eminently practical foundation on which the gospel rests. . . . Preaching is not the act of unfolding our personal convictions. It is the duty of informing men of all that God has spoken. To move off from the pages of Scripture is to enter into the wastelands of our own subjectivity.[3]

A Final Suggestion That Frees Us

There is much more to the Spirit's work within us than you and I have ever known or ever allowed ourselves to experience, but *do not be deceived*. Stay with God's Book of truth. Bounce everything off the written Word of God.

But as long as you keep the plumb line true, just remember that you may have a great deal of space between where you are and where the Spirit wants you to be.

Come nearer . . . don't be afraid to fly closer to the flame. It can revolutionize your prayer life, your daily witness, your own struggling, timid self-image, and for sure your confidence in God. It can give you strength and tranquility in the midst of sickness, even Stephen-like assurance in the face of death.

Ever since I started this book many months ago, an old hymn has been in my mind and on my lips:

I am thine, O Lord, I have heard Thy voice
And it told Thy love to me;
But I long to rise in the arms of faith,
And be closer drawn to Thee.

Consecrate me now to Thy service, Lord,
By the pow'r of grace divine;
Let my soul look up with a steadfast hope,
And my will be lost in Thine.

There are depths of love that I cannot know
Till I cross the narrow sea;
There are heights of joy that I may not reach
Till I rest in peace with Thee.

Draw me nearer, nearer, nearer, blessed Lord,
To the cross where Thou hast died;
Draw me nearer, nearer, nearer, blessed Lord,
To Thy precious, bleeding side.[4]

As I sang that grand old hymn in the shower last night, the thought crossed my mind: Must I wait until I get to "that narrow sea" before those intimate moments with God can be experienced? Must I wait until I "rest in peace with Thee" before I am able to reach such "heights of joy"? I used to think so. I don't anymore.

Lord, how grateful we are for this will of Yours, for this Word of Yours. Help us in the midst of the search to be kept from error. And while doing that, Lord, protect us as we fly closer to the flame. Take away the fear. Give us a holy boldness in faith. Stop us when we tend to run afraid of such new truths as this, but enable us to come closer and to listen better. And may we discover in the process a sweetness of relationship and a depth of intimacy with You such as we have never known before, all for Your glory. We "long to rise in the arms of faith" and be transformed by the power of your Spirit. So, draw us nearer, blessed Lord . . . nearer to You. In the Savior's dear name. Amen.

7

Those Unidentified Inner Promptings

$\mathcal{H}$AVE YOU EVER ATTENDED a UFO convention? I did once. Well, I didn't actually attend it, though I felt as if I had.

What happened was I was staying at the same hotel where some kind of UFO convention was being held. Every elevator was full of UFO devotees. Every line waiting for a cab, every meeting room, every restaurant table, even the lobby was choked with these folks. And let me tell you, some of those people are scary!

What took place during the day was wild enough, but after sunset things really got crazy. At all hours of the night you could see men and women in a nearby public park or standing near their windows or perched on hotel ledges—most of them with binoculars—scanning the stellar spaces and mumbling to each other. While one stared into the sky, looking for unidentified flying objects, another took notes, drawing diagrams and charts of whatever was being observed. Everywhere you looked there were little pockets of people pointing here and there, all excited about the things they were seeing in the night sky.

Funny, I never saw anything. Maybe I was too skeptical or too ignorant to know what to look for, but when I looked up, all I ever saw was your basic blue-black sky, moon, stars, and, every once in a while, clouds floating by.

I remember the first night in particular, when two people staying in the room next to mine on the ninth floor were so elated over what they saw they couldn't restrain their excitement. It was about half past two, maybe three o'clock in the morning when all the noise started. Finally, I crawled out of bed and went to my window. My lights were off, so I could get a better view. By the time I had sufficiently awakened and was able to stumble over to the window, they had gathered four or five other friends in their room and everybody was looking out the window, discussing how obviously visible something was in the distance. I peered out to where they were pointing. At first I thought there was something there and my pulse rate jumped a few notches, but then I realized it was only the light from the hotel hallway shining under the door and reflecting in my windowpane. I rubbed my eyes, squinted, and again scanned the sky very carefully. Honest . . . there was nothing there. Absolutely nothing.

That kind of stuff continued night after night all week long, and here I am, still waiting to spot my first UFO. Several months ago I really thought I saw one in the sky, toward the south of where I live here in Fullerton . . . but then it dawned on me that what I was getting excited over were the last few skyrockets from the nearby Disneyland fireworks finale. I'm still waiting to spot my first UFO.

Some well-meaning Christians remind me of those UFO people. They are always seeing what others can't see. They get all excited over stuff they experience . . . and when you don't, they make it sound like it's your fault! Because they are so sure they are right—and because so many like-minded, equally sincere folks are standing by nodding yes, yes, yes—very few have the courage to look them in the eye and say, "I don't see it!" Most of us just shrug our shoulders, roll our eyes, and let it pass.

Well, that may be okay when it comes to UFOs, but when it has to do with the things of the Spirit, it can't be shrugged off. Who really cares that much if a bunch of people claim to see spinning discs in the sky or futuristic wheels with bright lights flashing and weird-looking people with antennae sticking out of their heads climbing up and down ladders that glow in the dark? Most of that is so harmless it is humorous. But when strange sideshow tactics are carried out in the name of the living God . . . when multiple thousands (millions?) are being led astray from the truth, duped into investing their time and pouring their money into so-called ministries that promise "miracles" on a daily basis and extrabiblical supernatural "revelations" that keep the crowd coming, it's neither harmless nor humorous.

And so if you think I'm leaning in that direction by urging people to fly closer to the flame, I need to set the record straight. I am not. God's work is not done in a circus atmosphere. God's Spirit does not do stunts. And while I'm at it, God's true messengers don't offer supernatural directives that come from visions or trances. And their so-called prophecies aren't that at all. They are neither inspired nor reliable. Count on it—if it isn't between Genesis and Revelation, it is not divinely inspired, supernaturally infallible, or absolutely inerrant.

Quite frankly, you and I don't need more revelations from God; what we need is to observe and obey the truth that He has already revealed in His Book. God's Word is inerrant, absolute, and final.

My purpose for writing this volume, then, is not to suggest that we need new and fresh revelations from the Lord, but that we need to explore His Word and *expand our understanding of what He has already revealed* . . . which brings me to the subject of this chapter: Not UFOs but UIPs. What about all those "unidentified inner promptings" we tend either to ignore or misinterpret? Could they be connected in some way with the Spirit's working within us? Five come immediately to mind:

• You are experiencing an uneasy churning in the pit of your stomach. It is related to a decision you need to make, and you can't seem to figure it out. There is no specific biblical answer; either way you choose could be supported in the Scriptures. Interestingly, as you imagine going down one side of the fork in the road, the churning intensifies . . . but when you track the other side, it diminishes. You "sense" within yourself that that is what you should do, so you do it and it proves to be the right choice. We commonly call that "intuition" or more generally "finding God's will" . . . but is that unidentified inner prompting a part of the Spirit's working?

• You are spending time in God's Word. You are trying to discern what it means . . . what it is saying regarding a situation you are facing. The truth seems veiled, hidden from you. You are stumped. You begin to pray for enlightenment, for a much clearer understanding of His mind on this subject. You read the passage again and again. Suddenly, the whole picture develops clearly in your mind. You "see" it . . . you nod excitedly, knowing that you have unlocked the vault. You are able to grasp the meaning of what earlier seemed vague, perhaps even confusing. We call that "insight." In reality, why couldn't that be the supernatural inner prompting of the Spirit as He illuminates your understanding of God's Word and will? It isn't mere human insight, is it?

• You are going through a severe time of testing. Your heart is heavy . . . your mind preoccupied. The pain doesn't go away. Instead, you lose your appetite, you suffer from insomnia, you become increasingly more isolated, pensive, maybe a bit irritable. The heaviness hangs like an anchor. Often, tears come unexpectedly. And then, almost overnight, the ninety-five-pound weight is lifted off your chest. Amazingly, your turmoil subsides and a wonderful tranquility comes in its place. We commonly call that "relief," but is that all it is? Why couldn't this UIP be the direct result of the Spirit of God bringing supernatural comfort, inner healing, and a divine surge of peace?

• There is a growing sense of unrest and/or conflict between you and another person close to you. It could be with someone who works for you or with you. It might be a friend, a family member, or your partner in marriage. You wish things would change on their own, but they are only getting worse. Then, at just the right moment, using carefully chosen words, you address the issue(s) head-on. Good things happen as a result of the meeting; changes occur. We call it an "intervention," a time of serious confrontation. Yet couldn't this be the empowering of the Spirit? Might it not be His inner prompting, infusing you with the necessary courage to stand toe-to-toe with the person and talk straight about the problem?

• You are in a relationship with an individual who is becoming increasingly more difficult to deal with. Pressure mounts with each week that passes. It seems as though you won't be able to escape a showdown, though you doubt how beneficial such a verbal encounter would be. You pray fervently. Just when the situation reaches the unbearable stage, a turn of events occurs that completely removes the person from your life. You could not have orchestrated a more perfect arrangement of events, but the fact is you didn't actually do anything to put the scenario into motion. It just happened. We call that a "coincidence," but is that really what it was? Who's to say it wasn't another of those UIPs where God's sovereign Spirit stepped in and choreographed the whole thing, leaving you wonderfully affirmed and at ease?

We Are Fearfully and Wonderfully Made

When God created humanity, He put something of Himself in each of us. Unlike the beasts of the field or the birds of the sky or the blooming plants in the dirt, He placed within us His "image."

> And God created man in His own image, in the image of God
> He created him; male and female He created them.
> Genesis 1:27

That "image" sets human beings apart from all other living things on earth. With body, soul, and spirit, we are able to get in touch not only with our feelings, but with Him, our Creator. And, equally important, He is able to communicate with us. Unlike other creatures who operate their lives out of instinct, we are equipped with sufficient "internal machinery" to connect with the living God.

In fact, when we become children of God through faith in His Son, that connection with Him takes on a whole new dimension. As Paul wrote so clearly,

> For all who are being led by the Spirit of God, these are sons
> of God. For you have not received a spirit of slavery leading

to fear again, but you have received a spirit of adoption as
sons by which we cry out, "Abba! Father!" The Spirit Himself bears witness with our spirit that we are children of God.
Romans 8:14–16

Look closely at that concluding comment. God's Spirit literally communicates with—bears witness with—our inner being,
called here "our spirit." In other words, an entire system of inner
communication is established at the time of salvation, making it
possible for us to receive whatever it is the Spirit wishes to communicate!

The psalmist used another expression in describing our
uniqueness as human beings. In the magnificent Psalm 139 we are
told that the link between us and God's Spirit is not only a reality, it is inescapable:

> Where can I go from Thy Spirit?
> Or where can I flee from Thy presence?
> If I ascend to heaven, Thou art there;
> If I make my bed in Sheol, behold, Thou art there.
> If I take the wings of the dawn,
> If I dwell in the remotest part of the sea,
> Even there Thy hand will lead me,
> And Thy right hand will lay hold of me.
> Psalm 139:7–10

Wonderful, comforting thought: We and He are supernaturally interwoven and inseparable. Wherever you or I go, He goes.
Whatever we think, He knows. In fact, He oversaw our concep-
tion and He gave us our personality as well as our physical
makeup. The same psalm verifies this:

> For Thou didst form my inward parts;
> Thou didst weave me in my mother's womb.
> I will give thanks to Thee, for I am fearfully and
>   wonderfully made;
> Wonderful are Thy works.

And my soul knows it very well.
My frame was not hidden from Thee,
When I was made in secret,
And skillfully wrought in the depths of the earth.
Thine eyes have seen my unformed substance;
And in Thy book they were all written,
The days that were ordained for me,
When as yet there was not one of them.

Psalm 139:13–16

Don't miss that special line: "I am fearfully and wonderfully made." One Jewish commentator states, "Reflection upon the marvels of the human body, even with his elementary anatomical knowledge, inspired the Psalmist with awe and wonder."[1]

It's true. Caught up in the wonder of it all, the ancient writer exclaims how uniquely created we are. I suggest that uniqueness includes secret inner chambers and hidden capacities other created beings lack. I also would suggest that such an inner system provides for the reception of divine information and the understanding of biblical truths, unknown to the animal kingdom. By being "fearfully and wonderfully made," we are equipped to grasp the Spirit's messages as well as sense His compelling, awesome presence. That explains why we can hear His "still small voice" and decipher messages of peace or warning, conviction or guidance. God created us with that capacity.

In fact, a very familiar verse of Scripture points out how God's message can penetrate deep within us.

For the word of God is living and active and sharper than any two-edged sword, and piercing as far as the division of soul and spirit, of both joints and marrow, and able to judge the thoughts and intentions of the heart.

Hebrews 4:12

Don't hurry past those words just because you may be familiar with the verse. God's truths are able to enter into our "soul and spirit," exposing to us "the thoughts and intentions of the heart."

Amazing! As the Spirit ignites the fuel of God's written revelation, the flame bursts upon us and engulfs us with an inner awareness. No surgeon can operate on the soul or the inner spirit. That is the invisible realm where God's Spirit does His work. No matter how brilliant the neurologist may be, with all his knowledge of the brain and nervous system, he cannot touch the spirit within us. That is God's special abode. Medical men and women are able to understand gross anatomy—and the study of it is fascinating—but how little they know (and how little we know) of the soul and spirit . . . the inner realm where the Spirit of God dwells. That explains why you can be in the midst of recovery from major surgery and still experience no anxiety . . . because the Spirit of God is at work within you, bringing about that otherwise unidentified inner prompting of peace.

I hesitate to use this term, but this is all very *mysterious.* It is one of those examples of divine truth we cannot nail down and dissect with precision; however, we also cannot deny it. Every one of us in God's family has experienced at one time or another some inner prompting of the Spirit. We call them other things. We call them hunches or intuition. We call them premonitions. We call them flashes of insight. Or we may call them simply a sense of peace. In reality, however, all these things we identify in human terms are part of His working. Yet we so seldom connect these inner promptings with Him, and we somehow feel strange when we try to identify them. We shouldn't.

Inner Promptings Then and Now

Let's look at four biblical examples of the work of the Spirit . . . four occasions when the Spirit did a unique work in someone's life. And remember, if He did it then, He can do it today.

1. *In times of loneliness and desperation, the Spirit prompts hope and encouragement.*

The life of the prophet Elijah, a man intimately acquainted with the presence of God, provides strong evidence that "truth is stranger than fiction." The man stood alone before evil King Ahab and pronounced a drought. It didn't rain for three and a half years. During the time of that drought, God sent ravens to feed Elijah; every morning and evening they brought him bread and meat. When Elijah commanded the fire of God to fall on the altar that was flooded with water, the fire fell, to the amazement of the prophets of Baal, who were thereafter slain. Finally, on the heels of these and other great occasions of victory, when the prophet was most vulnerable, Jezebel, the wicked wife of King Ahab, threatened his life. The weary prophet couldn't handle it. He caved in.

> Now Ahab told Jezebel all that Elijah had done, and how he had killed all the prophets with the sword. Then Jezebel sent a messenger to Elijah, saying, "So may the gods do to me and even more, if I do not make your life as the life of one of them by tomorrow about this time." And he was afraid and arose and ran for his life and came to Beersheba, which belongs to Judah, and left his servant there. But he himself went a day's journey into the wilderness, and came and sat down under a juniper tree; and he requested for himself that he might die, and said, "It is enough; now, O LORD, take my life, for I am not better than my fathers."
>
> 1 Kings 19:1–4

Now ideally the prophet Elijah should have said, "Lord, I ask You to come down and be my protector, my very present help in this time of need. Calm my fears. Be my shield and my defender." But he didn't do that. Instead, he ran for his life and then slumped into a deep depression.

Deep in the woods, in an unusual moment of desperation, loneliness, and despair, Elijah sat down under a tree and asked the Lord to take his life. (Apparently the thought of suicide did not enter his mind.) Emotionally, physically, spiritually, he was at the bottom.

A more pathetic picture of heartbreaking loneliness can hardly be found in the Scriptures. There he sat, full of self-pity and disillusionment.

And what did God do? Our gracious God neither shamed him nor rebuked him; instead, with compassion and gentleness, He ministered to His servant.

> So He said, "Go forth, and stand on the mountain before the LORD." And behold, the LORD was passing by! And a great and strong wind was rending the mountains and breaking in pieces the rocks before the LORD; but the LORD was not in the wind. And after the wind an earthquake, but the LORD was not in the earthquake. And after the earthquake a fire, but the LORD was not in the fire; and after the fire a sound of a gentle blowing.
>
> 1 Kings 19:11–12

Let's pause right here. The old King James Version says that "after the fire" there was "a still, small voice." The New King James Bible renders it in a similar manner, but gives this footnote, "a delicate, whispering voice." The New International Version states that "after the fire came a gentle whisper." Can you picture the scene? Elijah, wrapped in his desolation, loneliness, and despair, is standing there in the howling wind, looking at the fire, feeling the earthquake. But the Lord was in none of it. And all of a sudden those phenomena subside and there is this "delicate whispering voice." Somehow, deep within the prophet's heart he hears something from God.

One reliable commentator states:

> It was not in the tempest that Jehovah was; . . . it was not in the earthquake that Jehovah was; . . . it was not in the fire that Jehovah was. . . . It was in a soft, gentle rustling that He revealed Himself to him [Elijah].[2]

I am unable to explain how Elijah sensed God's voice or exactly what the Spirit said, but clearly He connected with the prophet.

And what did Elijah do? Soon after that encounter with God, he wrapped himself in his mantle, and he moved toward the mouth of the cave. He didn't run from God; he moved toward Him.

I must admit, there have been times in my life when the Lord's promptings have been just as real to me as Elijah's experience was to him. No, I didn't hear an audible voice . . . I didn't see a vision . . . but His presence was so real I felt I could touch Him. Quite honestly, *it was magnificent*. Rather than being boisterous and bold, it was gentle and quiet . . . almost as if He were saying, "I have everything under control. Trust me. Depend on Me. Wait patiently for Me to work."

Now it is important to remember that some of the most profound ministries of the Spirit of God are not public or loud or large. Sometimes His most meaningful touch on our lives comes when we are all alone.

I urge you to include in your schedule time to be alone with God. I am fortunate to live within ninety minutes of the mountains . . . and less than forty-five minutes from the beach. Those are great places to commune with God. You do have places where you can get away for a long walk, don't you? I hope it's in a wooded area. The gentle breeze blowing through the forest is therapeutic. Sometimes just being alone out in God's marvelous creation is all that's needed for the scales to be removed from your eyes and for you to silence the harassment and the noise of your day and begin to hear from God. On those occasions the Lord ministers to us in a gentle whispering.

I took a walk in a forest some six thousand feet high a few weeks ago. There, all alone in the cold, surrounded by snow about a foot deep, I stood and leaned against a tree and poured out my heart to God. I must have done this for fifteen or twenty minutes . . . then I just listened. It was wonderful. Several things I had been concerned about fell into place there in His presence.

Scripture says, "Be still, and know that I am God." Elijah was still, and that was all he needed to find encouragement from the living God. Take time. Be still. Unload the weight of your soul. Listen.

2. In times of threatening fears, the Spirit prompts calm determination and courage.

Something Paul experienced in this regard during his third missionary journey is worth a second look.

> "And now, behold, bound in spirit, I am on my way to Jerusalem, not knowing what will happen to me there, except that the Holy Spirit solemnly testifies to me in every city, saying that bonds and afflictions await me. But I do not consider my life of any account as dear to myself, in order that I may finish my course, and the ministry which I received from the Lord Jesus, to testify solemnly of the gospel of the grace of God."
>
> Acts 20:22–24

This is a deeply emotional and moving account because the apostle is saying good-bye to his longtime friends from Ephesus. Adding to the emotion was the realization that he probably would not see them again.

Initially what I find interesting and intriguing is that Paul says he is "bound in the Spirit." I think he means that he is "bound by the Holy Spirit" rather than being tied up in knots within his own spirit. In other words, he was captured in thoughts of, surrounded by the presence of, unable to get away from the reminders of God's heaven-sent Helper. In some supernatural manner, the Spirit communicated with Paul's spirit as he "solemnly testified," saying, in effect, "You're in for trouble, Paul. No matter what city you enter, you are going to encounter intensified trouble." (That is exactly what happened.) A threatening fear could have seized him and sidetracked him. But it didn't. Why? Because Paul was not all that important to Paul. Remember what he wrote on another occasion?

> For to me, to live is Christ, and to die is gain. But if I am to live on in the flesh, this will mean fruitful labor for me; and I do not know which to chose.
>
> Philippians 1:21–22

Strictly from the human viewpoint, when you and I know that trouble and afflictions await us, we are frightened. That does not occur when the Spirit of God brings a sense of reassurance.

Could this not explain the relentless courage and determination of the martyrs and the missionaries of years gone by? If you're like me, when you read about their lives, you shake your head and think, "I cannot imagine how they endured such trials! How did they continue in such threatening times? How could they have not dreaded each dawn?" How? It was the Spirit of God! They were "bound in the Spirit" in the midst of those threatening fears.

Could this not explain the courage and determination of the Reformers? You read their stories and you realize how shallowly and superficially many of us live our lives. Though they lost reputation, occupation, status, and in some cases were burned at the stake, they stood resolute and confident. How could they do that? They were "bound in the Spirit."

When we fly closer to the flame, an unidentified inner prompting often says to our spirits, "I am here. I am aware of what you are going through. I know of the threats. I will take you through them." Perhaps the hymn writer knew of such divine promptings when he wrote those immortal lyrics:

> When through fiery trials thy pathway shall lie,
> My grace all-sufficient shall be thy supply;
> The flame shall not hurt thee; I only design
> Thy dross to consume, and thy gold to refine.[3]

A warning is appropriate here. This does not mean we presume on God, or are foolish and needlessly daring, or flirt with danger in the energy of the flesh. That is not the kind of courage we're talking about. What I am referring to is the remarkable way fear flees when the Spirit communicates His presence and gives us an "inner transfusion" of His incredible power.

3. *In times of potential danger and disaster, the Spirit prompts inner reassurance.*

One of the most exciting and adventuresome accounts in the New Testament is recorded in Acts 27. If you enjoy sailing, life on the open sea, the power of the wind and the waves, and the physical challenge of surviving a storm in the deep, you will love this chapter. It includes all that and more, as danger intensifies with each new scene.

> And when it was decided that we should sail for Italy, they proceeded to deliver Paul and some other prisoners to a centurion of the Augustan cohort named Julius. And embarking in an Adramyttian ship, which was about to sail to the regions along the coast of Asia, we put out to sea, accompanied by Aristarchus, a Macedonian of Thessalonica. And the next day we put in at Sidon; and Julius treated Paul with consideration and allowed him to go to his friends and receive care. And from there we put out to sea and sailed under the shelter of Cyprus because the winds were contrary. And when we had sailed through the sea along the coast of Cilicia and Pamphylia, we landed at Myra in Lycia. And there the centurion found an Alexandrian ship sailing for Italy, and he put us aboard it. And when we had sailed slowly for a good many days, and with difficulty had arrived off Cnidus, since the wind did not permit us to go farther, we sailed under the shelter of Crete, off Salmone; and with difficulty sailing past it we came to a certain place called Fair Havens, near which was the city of Lasea.
>
> And when considerable time had passed and the voyage was now dangerous. . . .
>
> Acts 27:1–9

Are you getting the picture? The seas are getting rougher. Dark storm clouds are gathering. The wind is whipping the sails. The currents are getting stronger. The old ship is groaning and creaking as it pitches and rolls in the angry Mediterranean. It's in the midst of this that Paul addresses those on the ship:

"Men, I perceive that the voyage will certainly be attended with damage and great loss, not only of the cargo and the ship, but also of our lives." But the centurion was more persuaded by the pilot and the captain of the ship, than by what was being said by Paul. And because the harbor was not suitable for wintering, the majority reached a decision to put out to sea from there, if somehow they could reach Phoenix, a harbor of Crete, facing southwest and northwest, and spend the winter there. And when a moderate south wind came up, supposing that they had gained their purpose, they weighed anchor and began sailing along Crete, close inshore. But before very long there rushed down from the land a violent wind, called Euraquilo; and when the ship was caught in it, and could not face the wind, we gave way to it, and let ourselves be driven along. And running under the shelter of a small island called Clauda, we were scarcely able to get the ship's boat under control. And after they had hoisted it up, they used supporting cables in undergirding the ship; and fearing that they might run aground on the shallows of Syrtis, they let down the sea anchor, and so let themselves be driven along. The next day as we were being violently storm-tossed, they began to jettison the cargo; and on the third day they threw the ship's tackle overboard with their own hands. And since neither sun nor stars appeared for many days, and no small storm was assailing us, from then on all hope of our being saved was gradually abandoned.

Acts 27:10–20

Have you ever been in a situation like that? Perhaps a howling blizzard or a tornado?

My brother Orville and his family endured Hurricane Andrew in South Florida. They listened as 150-mile-an-hour winds ripped off timbers and flung them through the house like spears. Doors were torn from their hinges and windows exploded. Both their cars were severely damaged. But in the midst of all this, Orville, his wife, and several others were crouched in the bedroom, praying. Incredibly, that room was the only room that suffered no damage. Anyone who lived through Hurricane Andrew can testify to its power, its danger, and to the disaster left in its wake.

It's a similar scene of danger here in Acts 27, and on top of everything else, those enduring it are at sea! They have already lost control, and now they begin losing their cargo. What most people fear in such situations, of course, is losing their life. And so, in the midst of this scene of panic, Paul addresses his shipmates and speaks with confidence, saying:

> "Men, you ought to have followed my advice and not to have set sail from Crete, and incurred this damage and loss. And yet now I urge you to keep up your courage, for there shall be no loss of life among you, but only of the ship.
>
> Acts 27:21–22

Question: How could he say that? Did he have some kind of premonition? The world may say so, but that's not the correct explanation. It is the work of the Spirit of God that gives this kind of courage. It doesn't come naturally. In the same way, how could my brother not panic in the midst of that hurricane with his precious family huddled around him? It was because the Spirit of God protected him and preserved him and gave him a sense of inner reassurance.

Paul verifies that his confidence came from the Lord. In fact, he says that he had been visited by an angel!

> "For this very night an angel of the God to whom I belong and whom I serve stood before me, saying, 'Do not be afraid, Paul; you must stand before Caesar; and behold, God has granted you all those who are sailing with you.' Therefore, keep up your courage, men, for I believe God, that it will turn out exactly as I have been told. But we must run aground on a certain island."
>
> Acts 27:23–26

His message was reassuring, but it was not unrealistic. Right up front he warned them that they would run aground. But not to worry . . . everyone would make it safely to shore. Read the closing scene and allow your imagination to run free:

But when the fourteenth night had come, as we were being driven about in the Adriatic Sea, about midnight the sailors began to surmise that they were approaching some land. And they took soundings, and found it to be twenty fathoms; and a little farther on they took another sounding and found it to be fifteen fathoms. And fearing that we might run aground somewhere on the rocks, they cast four anchors from the stern and wished for daybreak. And as the sailors were trying to escape from the ship, and had let down the ship's boat into the sea, on the pretense of intending to lay out anchors from the bow, Paul said to the centurion and to the soldiers, "Unless these men remain in the ship, you yourselves cannot be saved." Then the soldiers cut away the ropes of the ship's boat, and let it fall away. And until the day was about to dawn, Paul was encouraging them all to take some food, saying, "Today is the fourteenth day that you have been constantly watching and going without eating, having taken nothing. Therefore I encourage you to take some food, for this is for your preservation; for not a hair from the head of any of you shall perish." And having said this, he took bread and gave thanks to God in the presence of all; and he broke it and began to eat. And all of them were encouraged, and they themselves also took food. And all of us in the ship were two hundred and seventy-six persons. And when they had eaten enough, they began to lighten the ship by throwing out the wheat into the sea. And when day came, they could not recognize the land; but they did observe a certain bay with a beach, and they resolved to drive the ship onto it if they could. And casting off the anchors, they left them in the sea while at the same time they were loosening the ropes of the rudders, and hoisting the foresail to the wind, they were heading for the beach. But striking a reef where two seas met, they ran the vessel aground; and the prow stuck fast and remained immovable, but the stern began to be broken up by the force of the waves. And the soldiers' plan was to kill the prisoners, that none of them should swim away and escape; but the centurion, wanting to bring Paul safely through, kept them from their intention, and commanded that those who could swim should jump overboard first and get to land, and the rest should follow, some on planks, and others on various things from the ship. And thus it happened that they all were brought safely to land.

Acts 27:27–44

Note that all were ultimately present and accounted for. They were soaked, but safe . . . exactly as God had said.

How could Paul remain so encouraged? Because the Spirit of God, using an angelic messenger, prompted him to be confident in danger and to stand firm on that promise. Such events may indeed be rare—perhaps only once or twice in a lifetime. But my point is this: Paul wasn't merely a brave man who loved challenges. He was prompted by God to be of good courage, even though his circumstances were frightening. If you doubt that, it's been too long since you were at sea in a raging storm.

4. *In times of great sorrow and pain, the Spirit ministers grace to us.*

Tucked away in the first few verses of 2 Corinthians 12 is a classic example of God's ministry in the midst of human misery.

And because of the surpassing greatness of the revelations, for this reason, to keep me from exalting myself, there was given me a thorn in the flesh, a messenger of Satan to buffet me—to keep me from exalting myself! Concerning this I entreated the Lord three times that it might depart from me.

2 Corinthians 12:7–8

The writer is Paul, who admits to having a thorn in the flesh—probably some physical ailment that brought excruciating, unrelenting pain. And so, naturally, he asked the Lord to bring relief . . . but relief didn't come. On three separate occasions he prayed that God would take away the pain. All three times the answer was the same. "No." But then God communicated something to Paul's inner spirit that brought him an enormous sense of relief. I call this message another of the Spirit's "inner promptings." And what was it God made known to Paul in his pain?

> And He has said to me, "My grace is sufficient for you, for power is perfected in weakness."
>
> 2 Corinthians 12:9

Grace. The God of all grace ministered grace to His hurting servant. Grace to endure. Grace to handle the pain. Grace to face the future. Grace to accept God's no. What a profound impact that had on the man!

> Most gladly, therefore, I will rather boast about my weaknesses, that the power of Christ may dwell in me. Therefore I am well content with weaknesses, with insults, with distresses, with persecutions, with difficulties, for Christ's sake; for when I am weak, then I am strong.
>
> 2 Corinthians 12:9b–10

I write from firsthand experience in this matter. I can't tell you the number of times God's power has been perfected and revealed in my own weakness. Some messages that I have received from God's Word and delivered in times of enormous weakness and inadequacy in my own life have been messages most blessed of God. I struggled through them, didn't feel like anybody would even want to listen, and couldn't wait to get out of the places where I was teaching or preaching because of my own disappointment or struggle at the time. But later I heard response after response telling how God had used those words in the lives of listeners.

When the Spirit of the Lord ministers grace, He prompts within us an unusual measure of divine strength. Somehow, in the mystery of His plan, He turns our pain into a platform upon which He does some of His best work.

Two Practical Suggestions

From UFOs to Mediterranean shipwrecks, we have covered a lot of ground in this chapter. So let me just add a couple of suggestions to help us keep our balance through all this.

First, *when you are not sure that something is from the Spirit, tread softly.* Back off. Use the Scriptures as your guide. If they are of the Lord, those unidentified inner promptings won't contradict anything biblically. Peace will remain your companion. The Lord doesn't lead against His own revealed Word. So don't get on a hobbyhorse over something that is questionable or clearly unbiblical.

Second, *when you are confident that it's of God, stand firm, even against other people's doubts.* Be strong and resolute. That's a part of walking by faith. There are times when other people will say, "There is no way in the world God could be in this"; yet you know absolutely in your heart that He is. At times like that, simply stand firm. You won't be able to convince them, but that's all right. God is still doing unusual things. BUT don't get weird. You can be confident in God without becoming spooky or seeing lots of things no one else can see.

Which reminds me, if I ever run into you at a UFO convention, you and I are going to have a talk.

8

The Spirit and Our Emotions

"Don't slam the door."

"Eat everything on your plate."

"Say ma'am and sir."

"Don't run inside the house."

"Keep your shoes shined."

"Don't talk with your mouth full."

"Work first, play later."

Sound familiar? Those are some of the rules by which I was raised. You can probably identify with one or two. Most families have them . . . you know, mottoes to live by.

Another that stands out in my mind was one of my mother's favorites: "You can't trust your feelings." To this day I can clearly recall her words as she warned us kids against relying on our emotions: "What you really want, son, are the facts. Facts are your friends . . . feelings will change on you."

As I grew up and became a Christian, this attitude was affirmed again and again. In the churches I attended, the pastors warned against "getting too emotional." Teachers in Sunday school agreed. If you're looking for something to give substance to your faith, they said, stay with the facts, not your feelings. Later, as I got under way in seminary, the same axiom was drilled into my head. Start with the facts. Make them the building blocks of your theology. Then, on the basis of those facts, live by faith. Your feelings will fall in line. Often, feelings were treated as if they either didn't exist or, if they did, were not important, sort of like second-class citizens. Just ignore your feelings; they'll fall in line . . . they'll catch up.

I am not alone in this experience. One writer puts it this way:

> In my youth as a Christian I was greatly helped by the story about Faith, Feelings, and Facts, companions together along a tricky pathway. The first two followed Facts who was in the lead. The story taught me that objective truth (Facts) was what mattered, and that my eyes of faith should be pinned on the facts, rather than on my emotions.
>
> Mr. Faith, you may remember, was often bothered when Mr. Feelings got into difficulties. However, when he took his eyes off Facts and turned to help Mr. Feelings, he himself invariably got into difficulties until he remembered that his job was to follow Facts, not to worry about Feelings. And according to the story, sooner or later Feelings would catch up.
>
> The story teaches both a truth and a lie. The truth is that our faith is based on facts, not on feelings. The lie was that feelings always caught up.[1]

How true! Our faith is based on facts—rock-solid, reliable, essential facts—not feelings.

It is not true, however, that our feelings always catch up.

Something else bothers me about this, too, and that is all the things I have been taught against feelings . . . almost as if emotions are spurious, never reliable, hardly worth mentioning. And even worse, it is as if emotions are never prompted by the Spirit of God . . . that they are far removed from anything connected with true spirituality.

Where did we get such an idea? Since when is the Spirit's work limited to our minds and our wills but not our hearts? Why is it that so many of us Evangelicals are so afraid of feelings? What has happened to us? Why must our theology and the expression of our faith be devoid of emotion? After all, God made us whole people; He created us with minds, wills, and hearts. And if He created us with the capacity to feel, shouldn't we be free to talk about our feelings, to express them, and to value them in ourselves and in others?

Rather than their being unimportant, I have found that my feelings often represent some of the most sensitive areas in my life touched by the Spirit of God. Not infrequently do my emotions play a vital role in how and where the Spirit is guiding me, giving me reasons to make significant decisions, cautioning me to back off, and reproving me for something in my life that needs immediate attention.

How else but through feelings do we experience that "peace that passes understanding"? Peace is, in the final analysis, an emotion.

How else but through feelings can we sense the presence of evil and the dangers of subtle temptations? Uneasy warning signals within us are actually emotional reactions, aren't they?

How else but through feelings are we prompted to "rejoice with those who rejoice, and weep with those who weep" (Rom. 12:15)?

And when we give God our praise, is it not from the depths of our emotions?

Don't feelings play a prominent role in our acts of righteous indignation, as well as in maintaining a positive attitude toward suffering, rejoicing in the Lord, loving others, and giving thanks in everything?

All these are things the Lord commands us to do; yet we could not obey apart from the release of our emotions. Strangely, however, many believers are still hesitant to let them out; they still "don't trust their feelings."

We are strange creatures: proud of our brains, stubborn in our wills, but ashamed of our emotions—though we deny all three! One of the many benefits of flying closer to the flame is that it allows us to warm up to our emotions, which is nothing more than allowing ourselves the freedom to be real, to be whole.

I have seen some incredible things in my adult life that illustrate the absence of this. Like a friend of mine who lost his wife after a long and bitter bout with cancer. He watched her in the downward-spiraling process survive several major surgeries, endure the humiliating experiences connected with chemo-therapy, and literally become a living skeleton. Even though the whole tragedy was agony for her and heartbreaking for him, he never once broke—even when death finally came as a long-awaited relief. He never admitted to me his own emotional ex-haustion, feelings of grief over losing his lovely wife, anger at the disease, or questions that surely haunted him in the middle of those nights.

Instead, he always maintained a calm, quiet acceptance, quoted several verses of Scripture, and even smiled with gratitude over others' concern for his wife's welfare. As I would press him for how he must be feeling—the loneliness, the awful struggle, the helplessness of watching his beloved slipping from his arms—there was never a tear, never a crack in his countenance. Even at the memorial service in her honor he was busy comforting others in-stead of being crushed by his own grief. While I heard a few ad-mirable comments about how strong he was through it all—"like the rock of Gibraltar," someone whispered—I found myself in-creasingly more concerned over his lack of emotion . . . his in-ability to admit his grief and genuinely mourn her death. I still wonder if he thought that his reaction was "the proper Christian response" so he dared not let those real feelings show.

Becoming a Christian is not synonymous with becoming superhuman. Expressing one's emotions is not a mark of imma-turity or carnality. The loss of a loved one is just as much a loss for the believer as it is for the nonbeliever. A killer disease like cancer—especially in its final stages—arouses the same feelings in the Christian's heart as in the heart without Christ. Pain is pain. Loss is loss. Death is death. At such times tears are not only ac-ceptable, they are appropriate and expected. It is part of being real, being human. Nothing is gained by denial or proven by remaining stoic.

The apostle Paul did not write that Christians are not to grieve, but that we do not grieve as if we "have no hope" (1 Thess. 4:13). There should be a lot of room in our theology for feelings of loss and tears, just as there is room for lighthearted, joyous feelings and great laughter. The Spirit of God prompts both. I have been concerned for years that too many so-called mature evangelical Christians have little room in their lives for either . . . which reminds me of another "rule" repeated in too many Christian homes: "Do not cry . . . it's a sign of weakness." Will somebody please point out to me where that is found in the Scriptures?

God Has Made Us "Whole People"

Speaking of the Scriptures, let's take a look at when and how God created humanity. And in doing so, let's pay close attention to how man and woman differ from planets and plants, fish and fowl. This search takes us all the way back to Creation, recorded in Genesis 1 and 2.

Genesis 1 is a general survey of the great Creation, beginning with the opening words of the Bible:

> In the beginning God created the heavens and the earth. And the earth was formless and void, and darkness was over the surface of the deep; and the Spirit of God was moving over the surface of the waters.
>
> Genesis 1:1–2

God was directly engaged in the whole creative activity and, interestingly, the Spirit of God was equally active, hovering over (literally) the process. As we read through this chapter we discover the divine plan being worked out miraculously and meticulously. From one *day* to the next, from one *category* to the next, life is being created and established—vegetation, birds, fish, animals, reptiles—it's all there, unfolding from God's fiat word and creative power.

Finally, the time arrives for the creation of humans. The Godhead—Father, Son, Spirit—agrees that this category will be unique:

> Then God said, "Let Us make man in Our image, according
> to Our likeness . . ."
>
> Genesis 1:26

Intriguing words, "Our image . . . Our likeness." The following verse verifies precisely what transpired:

> And God created man in His own image, in the image of God
> He created him; male and female He created them.
>
> Genesis 1:27

Twice the inspired record states that, unlike all other created life, mankind bears the "image" of the Creator. Plant life does not have this "image," nor do the birds of the air, the fish of the sea, or the beasts of the field. Only mankind.

And what is that "image"? Volumes have been written by theologians attempting to answer that question. Rather than getting involved in such a detailed analysis, let me summarize my answer by using the words *personality* and *nature*. God gave humanity a personality, or nature, like His own.

God has a "mind"—intellect. When He created Adam and Eve, God gave them the same. He gave them an intelligence that was higher than other created life. This is illustrated not only in the command to "rule over the fish . . . the birds . . . the cattle and over all the earth" (Gen. 1:26), but also in Adam's naming all the creatures God had created (Gen. 2:19). The first man and woman were able to communicate with each other verbally, to make observations about one another, and to understand their Creator's instructions—all characteristics of intelligence. Ultimately, they were given this kind of mind that they might know their God.

God has a "heart"—emotions. When He created Adam and Eve, God gave them the same. Their emotional makeup and capacity were unique. Combined with their intellect, they could feel what no other created life could feel. The full spectrum of emotions was there for them to experience . . . from intense affection and exuberant joy to intense anger; they could feel disappointment, sadness, comfort, refreshment, excitement, and ecstasy. All this and so much more were theirs at creation. Adam's delight in seeing Eve for the first time (Gen. 2:23) is a good example of his emotions. A literal reading of that verse suggests that he burst forth with strong feelings of excitement when God brought her to him for the first time: "Now—at last!" And their intimate joy in marital love offers yet another example of their capacity to feel deeply (Gen. 2:25). Ultimately, Adam and Eve were given emotions that they might love their God.

God has a "will"—volition. When He created the first couple, God gave them the same. Nothing else in creation had this ability. Mixed with their intellectual and emotional capacities, this volitional ability enabled Adam and Eve to understand and reason things through, feel the emotions of the issues, then make decisions and act upon them. God appealed to Adam's will when He gave him commands, like:

> "From any tree of the garden you may eat freely; but from the tree of the knowledge of good and evil you shall not eat, for in the day that you eat from it you shall surely die."
>
> Genesis 2:16–17

God gave Adam and Eve a will that they might obey their God.

The Significant Presence of Our Feelings

Let's spend a few minutes on some of the salient emotions that are a part of our God-given personality. Though it may come as a surprise to some Christians who have never felt the freedom to acknowledge and to affirm their emotions, the New Testament is full of comments regarding the presence of feelings. Two verses from the Corinthian letters come to mind:

But just as it is written,

> "THINGS WHICH EYE HAS NOT SEEN AND
>   EAR HAS NOT HEARD,
> AND WHICH HAVE NOT ENTERED THE
>   HEART OF MAN,
> ALL THAT GOD HAS PREPARED FOR THOSE
>   WHO LOVE HIM."

1 Corinthians 2:9

For God, who said, "Light shall shine out of darkness," is the One who has shone in our hearts to give the light of the knowledge of the glory of God in the face of Christ.

2 Corinthians 4:6

God's work in salvation is directed to the heart, not just the mind. When the Lord begins His saving work in the life of the sinner, He goes right to the heart!

Interesting, isn't it? Entering into the heart, targeting the emotions of the sinner, the Lord begins His persuasive convincing. When a person chooses to reject the things of God, it means that those things have not entered into his or her *heart*. The mind of that unredeemed one is blinded, yes, but the heart is also untouched . . . unconvinced . . . unmoved.

This helps explain why so much is said in Scripture regarding a hard heart, a dull heart, a calloused heart. The Pharaoh in Moses' day comes to mind. In spite of all that happened, all the misery of the plagues and all the evidence he witnessed, his heart remained unmoved. The stubborn Egyptian leader remained hard of heart. The Spirit of God never invaded and took His rightful place on the seat of his emotions.

If you are saved, part of the reason God got your attention and came into your life is that He reached your heart and He softened your feelings toward Him.

Paul testifies that his own heart's passion was for the salvation of his fellow Jews.

Brethren, my heart's desire and my prayer to God for them
is for their salvation.

Romans 10:1

He later writes that genuine salvation occurs not simply because we say so, but because we have a heartfelt belief.

That if you confess with your mouth Jesus as Lord, and believe in your heart that God raised Him from the dead, you
shall be saved; for with the heart man believes, resulting in
righteousness, and with the mouth he confesses, resulting in
salvation.

Romans 10:9–10

Obviously this use of the word *heart* is broader than just a
reference to the emotions, but it would certainly include such.

I would challenge you to do a study of your own on the
emotions mentioned in the New Testament. If you do, you will
be amazed at the number of feelings—human, everyday feelings—God underscores. In some cases He prompts them; in
others, He works through them or He speaks to them. They are
interwoven through the entire fabric of truth. Let me mention
several examples:

Joy and Cheer

Now this I say, he who sows sparingly shall also reap
sparingly; and he who sows bountifully shall also reap bountifully.

2 Corinthians 9:6

Using a vivid illustration from the world of agriculture, Paul
writes that a light sowing will result in a light harvest, while a
generous sowing will yield a generous harvest. He then applies
this to the contributing of one's money to God's eternal work
on earth:

> Let each one do just as he has purposed in his heart; not grudgingly or under compulsion; for God loves a cheerful giver.
>
> 2 Corinthians 9:7

I find it interesting that we purpose to give in our heart—another example of volition teaming up with emotions. When we give as we should, for all the right reasons, we are "cheerful." In fact, the Greek term so translated is the word from which we get "hilarious."

Love

Look next at 2 Timothy 1:7:

> For God has not given us a spirit of timidity, but of power and love and discipline.

Two opposite emotions are mentioned here: One is not prompted by God (timidity, or cowardice), and the other one is (love). If there is one word that could easily be the theme of the New Testament, it would be *love* (*agape*). This particular term is a uniquely Christian word, indicating an active pursuit in seeking the highest good of another. *Agape* appears frequently in John's writings, especially the letter of 1 John, where we find the verse that is a favorite of many:

> We love, because He first loved us.
>
> 1 John 4:19

Fear

I mentioned this emotion earlier, but it would be helpful to underscore it by going back into the Old Testament and seeing it clearly in the ancient book of wisdom, the Proverbs:

> The fear of the LORD is the beginning of knowledge.
>
> Proverbs 1:7

God honors such feelings of "fear," a term that suggests an awesome respect for our Lord with an accompanying hatred for sin. This does not mean that we are frightened by God, but that we have a holy respect for Him . . . so great that sin is allowed no place in our conscious life.

Praise

At least eleven of the psalms, including the last five, begin with the same words: "Praise the Lord!" This is not simply an intellectual response based on facts. It is an emotional act of worship, praising and extolling the living God. Praise includes deep feelings of adoration and heartfelt affection, and God honors those spontaneous "bursts" of our adoration.

Other Feelings

Joy . . . love . . . fear . . . praise . . . those are basic and very powerful emotions. Yet they are only a few of the many emotions referred to in Scripture as an integral part of our spiritual lives. For example, in the section of Scripture that follows—just one section—note how many of these commands involve feelings generated within our hearts:

> Let love be without hypocrisy. Abhor what is evil; cling to what is good. Be devoted to one another in brotherly love; give preference to one another in honor; not lagging behind in diligence, fervent in spirit, serving the Lord; rejoicing in hope, persevering in tribulation, devoted to prayer, contributing to the needs of the saints, practicing hospitality. Bless those who persecute you; bless and curse not. Rejoice with those who rejoice, and weep with those who weep. Be of the same mind toward one another; do not be haughty in mind, but associate with the lowly. Do not be wise in your own estimation. Never pay back evil for evil to anyone. Respect what is right in the sight of all men. If possible, so far as it depends on you, be at peace with all men.
> Romans 12:9–18

Thinking of strong emotions, I am particularly drawn to those lines that state that when our brothers and sisters hurt, we hurt . . . we "weep with those who weep." Those are deep feelings that come from the Spirit of God, who is Himself moved over our sorrow.

While my wife and I were traveling abroad, we got word through a fax that two of her longtime, closest friends were seriously ill. One was in the final stage of her battle with cancer (she has recently died), and the other had had a massive stroke. I stood near and watched my wife as she read this message. Before she could even finish reading the words on that sheet, she broke into tears. A piece of paper communicated information from across the ocean, giving only a brief account of two good friends, but that was sufficient to cause her to sob. I took her into my arms and held her close as the Spirit of God "hovered over" her emotions while her heart was breaking. Miles separated her from these two friends she loved deeply. She was unable to be there, to touch them, to talk to them, to stroke their hair, or to embrace them. But she was able to cry her heart out as she felt the pain of loss, helplessness, and grief. The deep feeling she expressed came from the Spirit of God.

Unusual Feelings

Have you ever been annoyed with someone else? Yes, I'm sure everyone has. Let me show you how even that can come from God's Spirit. I'm thinking of an account in Acts 17 that records an incident that occurred during Paul's second missionary journey. The apostle had been engaged in evangelism up in Macedonia, and when he came down into Greece, he waited for his friends Silas and Timothy at Athens. And . . .

> while Paul was waiting for them at Athens, his spirit was being provoked within him as he was beholding the city full of idols.
>
> Acts 17:16

It has been said that in those days there were more idols in Athens than there were people. Imagine that. Such an overwhelming presence of idolatry "provoked" Paul, and that emotion became the spark that lit the fire in his belly. Deep within his soul he was burdened about the condition of that city. God gave him those feelings. The result?

> So he was reasoning in the synagogue with the Jews and the God-fearing Gentiles, and in the market place every day with those who happened to be present.
>
> Acts 17:17

Another unusual account appears in Acts 19, during the evangelization of Ephesus, a city of prominence in the first century. It was, however, a city given over to superstition and idolatry. So we shouldn't be surprised to read:

> And God was performing extraordinary miracles by the hands of Paul, so that handkerchiefs or aprons were even carried from his body to the sick, and the diseases left them and the evil spirits went out. But also some of the Jewish exorcists, who went from place to place, attempted to name over those who had the evil spirits the name of the Lord Jesus, saying, "I adjure you by Jesus whom Paul preaches." And seven sons of one Sceva, a Jewish chief priest, were doing this. And the evil spirit answered and said to them, "I recognize Jesus, and I know about Paul, but who are you?" And the man, in whom was the evil spirit, leaped on them and subdued all of them and overpowered them, so that they fled out of that house naked and wounded. And this became known to all, both Jews and Greeks, who lived in Ephesus; and fear fell upon them all and the name of the Lord Jesus was being magnified. Many also of those who had believed kept coming, confessing and disclosing their practices. And many of those who practiced magic brought their books together and began burning them in the sight of all; and they counted up the price of them and found it fifty thousand pieces of silver.

So the word of the Lord was growing mightily and prevailing.
Acts 19:11–20

What an incredible account! But so it goes when God's work is taking place and the enemy is being confronted. Isn't it interesting that the people were led to confess their secret lives and disclose their private practices of evil?

Have you ever been in a revival like that? I have seen it happen. I have witnessed occasions when the Spirit of God does such an effective work of cleansing that people can no longer contain their secret sins. When the Spirit works on the emotions of a person, hearts that were once calloused and hardened are softened, breeding a respect for God and a hatred of sin.

You may have known people who used to express their emotions and were colorful, enthusiastic types, stimulating to be around; then, because of an accident or a disease or a stroke, those same people became emotionally "deadened." The contrast is remarkable! I am thinking of a young man who was in a terrible auto accident. The lack of oxygen to his brain during his recovery precipitated damage that robbed him of his emotions. Prior to that tragic series of events, he was a quick, exciting, fun-loving, and responsive fellow everyone enjoyed being around. Today, his "emotionless" condition is heartbreaking to behold. When his father died several months ago, he communicated the fact to me—the day after it happened—with no more feeling than if he were mentioning the time of day or the weather that afternoon.

Though it may seem a quantum leap of comparison, I have witnessed a similar loss of emotion among those who enter seminary! Many enter those classrooms of theological learning full of zeal for the lost, a warm-hearted hunger for God, and a teachable, humble spirit. But unhappily, years later, many leave with an altogether different attitude and spirit. Something strange occurs during those years in the cloistered halls and under piles of books in the library. Instead of falling more deeply in love with Christ and others in the body, many seem to fall in love with learning and slowly slip out of touch with reality. Theological discussions and debates become more stimulating than being with real-world people and ministering to real-world needs. Instead of those seminary years heightening their enthusiasm, it kills it; instead of their growing knowledge of God humbling them further and making them aware of their own ignorance, it puffs them up, making them aloof, heady, dull, and dry. (If you think I'm exaggerating, ask their wives . . . visit with their children!)

This need not be, and it certainly is not the fault of learning theology, as some would suggest. And, I am exceedingly delighted to add, for some this emotional erosion never occurs. They remain warm, in touch, and gracious men and women of God. The problem rests with the learner, who substitutes theory for reality . . . and discounts the value of remaining balanced in mind and heart.

Some Necessary Warnings We Need to Heed

This is a good time for me to pause and mention three basic warnings so that our flying closer to the flame will take place without fear of getting our wings singed.

Intellectualism

Intellectualism is what we have just been talking about, but it is not reserved for seminary students. It can occur whenever we refuse to allow our emotions to serve their proper function. By holding them in constant check, by restraining the natural flow of our feelings, we can begin to rely strictly on the intellect for our walk with Christ. As Paul states so clearly, "knowledge makes arrogant" (1 Cor. 8:1).

In schools or churches where the Bible becomes a textbook for learning facts to the exclusion of having one's heart warmed and one's life changed, intellectualism crouches at the door, ready to seize its victims. It reminds me of the oft-heard warning: "Be careful that going to Bible school or seminary doesn't damage your faith!" It would probably be discouraging to know how many do lose their faith in the midst of a sterile, intellectual climate.

If we hope to counteract intellectualism, there must always be Spirit-filled warmth and a climate of devotion to the person of Christ. Staying real helps.

Emotionalism

This occurs when we go to the other extreme, making emotions the heart and center of life. Emotionalism results when one builds one's faith on the sands of experience rather than on the solid, reliable rock of faith based on facts. A life of solid faith starts with a clear understanding of biblical doctrine. Balance calls for both mind and heart . . . in that order. They need to be woven together carefully, slowly, and correctly like a God-given tapestry.

Fanaticism

Fanaticism occurs in a context of excessive and intense devotion to information that lacks balance, discernment, and wisdom. Fanatics become so enthralled with a teaching that the mind focuses solely on that while the emotions take control and one's actions become bizarre and unhealthy.

A classic example would be falling into the bondage of one of the cults. In these instances, a single authority figure requires blind loyalty. That person is not accountable or open to criticism or correction, and this exclusive spirit is often accompanied by paranoid reactions. There is an unwholesome lack of balance—including the absence of a healthy sense of humor—and the inability to enter into a broad spectrum of interests and activities.

This, of course, is not limited to the cults. Any one of us is able to fall into extremes and become fanatical, losing ourself in certain intense pursuits.

Convinced that that interest is the *only interest* worth pursuing, we can then become impatient with others because they are not as charged up as they should be about *our* single-minded concern. At that point our emotions get out of control, fuel the fire of zeal, and shout, "Full speed ahead!" This explains why fanatics become offensive without knowing it and how they can ignore basic responsibilities of life without concern. The subjects can be (and usually are) religious or doctrinal in nature, such as prophecy, the gifts of the Spirit, witnessing, prayer, legalism, freedom, knowledge (as an end in itself), some social concern, and a hundred other possibilities.

Be warned! When the Spirit of God is not in full control, there is the tendency in all of us—*and that includes you*—to go haywire emotionally. Wise are those who keep their balance . . . even when flying closer to the flame. Correction: *especially* when flying closer to the flame.

Some Traditional Sayings We Need to Clarify

I want to close this chapter by clarifying some traditional sayings. Since we started this chapter by mentioning a very common one, let me return to it first.

Never trust your feelings. As I said earlier, many of us were raised on that statement. But I think it needs to be tempered. It is the word *never* that I stumble over. Since peace, which is an emotion, is a part of the inner affirmation that God gives us when we are in the nucleus of His will, you and I *better* trust it! If you aren't comfortable with the word *trust,* then how about *being open* to it? We are instructed to "let the peace of Christ rule in your hearts" (Col. 3:15), so we certainly must give peace its due.

Another feeling we hear little about in Christian circles is intuition. This is the ability to perceive or know something without conscious reasoning. It is a very private emotion. Something inside of you churns, saying, "No, I wouldn't do that." Or it smiles and says, "Yes, this is good. This is what you ought to do—or at least *consider* doing."

One man tells me that he has learned over the years that the best way to lead his business is by intuitive leading. "I just know in my spirit when something is right or something is wrong," he says. And in case you are wondering, his business is doing exceedingly well.

To be sure, there needs to be seasoned wisdom along with keen discernment if we hope to operate intuitively. But even though it is a feeling, trusting is not all bad. There are times we *better* trust our feelings.

Experience proves nothing is another traditional saying. In fact, I used to say that myself, but I'm not nearly as dogmatic as I used to be. I have lived long enough to know that there are times when experience is extremely valuable and can certainly prove something. Something I experienced years ago comes to mind.

I have the dubious record of holding one of the shortest pastorates in the history of the church: I was the pastor of a church for less than twelve hours! Let me explain.

I was serving in one church when another church in a nearby city began pursuing me. I wasn't looking to change pastorates at that time, but they were interested in me. So Cynthia and I prayed and discussed the possibility, and I decided to look deeper into the situation. I had dinner with the chairman of the board, I got counsel from a few friends, and I thought carefully through the process. Finally, after I had spent some time with their board, I candidated. When we came to the night for the congregational vote, they voted yes. Everyone seemed delighted, including Cynthia and me.

As I recall, it was a unanimous vote. That's the way it ought to be, I thought, as Cynthia and I drove home late that evening. Yet I felt I should be more excited than I was, and I didn't say much to Cynthia in the car. She started talking about how we would need to sell our home and find another place to live. I said less and less. Once we got home I told her I was exhausted and dropped into bed . . . but sleep didn't come. My mind was whirling. I was miserable. Finally, shortly after dawn, I telephoned the chairman of the board.

"Bill?"

"Yes."

"Hey, I'm not coming."

"You're not what? You told us last night—"

"I know . . . I know. I have been your pastor for less than twelve hours. I'm no longer the pastor. The answer is no."

"Why?"

"I just don't feel right about it, Bill."

"Well, maybe we ought to talk about it."

And I knew we could talk about it until kingdom come, but I would not be changing my mind because I knew I should not go. I can't explain that. You know what it was? Primarily, my response was based on a series of feelings. I experienced a growing uneasiness, and I learned how valuable such an emotion can be. It was right! And I am so glad I finally submitted to my feelings.

That entire (somewhat embarrassing) experience proved something to me: that I can think at the moment something is right and later realize it is wrong.

Many years ago I had a woman say to me, "I remember saying to my father as I was walking down the aisle with him at my wedding, 'Daddy, I should not be here doing this.' And my daddy said, 'Keep walking, honey. Keep walking.'"

I am sure her father meant well, but that was the wrong answer. The marriage didn't last. Her feelings were right.

Now I know that feelings of panic often surface when one thinks about taking that final step toward marriage. But this young woman felt a deep inner reluctance . . . something was telling her that she should not be walking down that aisle, she should not be getting married to that man. Great guy. Fine gal. But not good for each other.

I understand uneasy feelings connected with weddings. I have had grooms almost vomit thinking about walking down the aisle. So we talk about it. Around 99 percent of the time, he's just nervous. But if a bride or groom is *really* sure it ought not to happen . . . cancel! Pay attention to feelings like that.

Such experiences can prove many things!

When it comes to experience, tradition also says: *Experience is the best teacher.* Let me add a word to that, and I'll accept the statement. *Guided* experience is the best teacher.

Experience alone is not the best teacher, but when we have been guided by someone who is reliable, it is the best teacher. If you don't agree with that, try laying a brick wall. I can always tell when I am standing next to a first-experience, homemade wall. The guy is always proud of it, but it looks horrible. If we want experience to teach its best lessons, having a guide helps.

Finally, tradition says: *Let your conscience be your guide.* Well, it all depends on the condition of your conscience! Sometimes one's conscience is reliable, sometimes not.

Conscience is like a compass. If a compass is faulty, you'll quickly get off course. A conscience gets its signals from the heart, which can be dulled, hardened, or calloused. Furthermore, a conscience can be overly sensitive or can even drive one mad.

Someone who has been reared by legalistic parents who used guilt and shame to manipulate their children often has a conscience that is overly sensitive. Some have consciences so twisted and confused, they need extensive help before they can start thinking correctly. Sometimes it takes the help of a good Christian therapist . . . someone who can help an individual with a shame-based conscience to understand how things got all fouled up. Sometimes a long-term friendship helps give grace to a conscience that has known only legalism. A conscience that is legalistic is not a good guide. A libertine conscience is not a good guide either, nor is a calloused conscience.

In order for one's conscience to be a good guide, one the Spirit can direct, it needs to be healthy, sensitive, and capable of getting God's message and truth.

This is a good time to add that the message of Christ is not devoid of emotions. When one realizes the true condition of the heart without God and ponders the impact of his or her sinfulness, there is an emotional reaction—greater in some than in others.

But there is an emotional reaction. *I have offended. I have grieved the heart of God. I have driven nails into Christ's hands with my sins.* That does something to my emotions when I, as a sinner, realize that. When the truth of forgiveness and grace and God's overwhelming love pour over me, there is an emotional reaction. And I must admit that. When I realize that God has reserved a home in heaven for me—a reprobate sinner who was running in the other direction when He stopped me, turned me around in grace, and brought me to Himself—that brings an emotional response. Don't deny those emotions!

And there are emotions on the journey from earth to heaven. When we come to the deathbed of a loved one, for example, feelings stream out as we think of that person's earthly departure . . . feelings of our loss on this earth . . . feelings of joy for them in heaven. Again, don't deny those feelings!

The music of the gospel is rich with emotion. Without those feelings, such music becomes little more than a professional performance. The message of the gospel is to be delivered with emotion, not just intellect. Otherwise, it becomes little more than a lecture. Church gatherings that restrain Spirit-led emotions can become dull and routine, perfunctory, lacking excitement, encouragement, and enlightenment.

God gave you a mind. Use it to know Him better. Study the doctrines that put steel into the cement of your faith. Exercise your mind!

God gave you a will. Use it to obey Him. Make decisions that honor Him and please Him. Exercise your will!

And God gave you emotions. Don't be afraid of them. Let them out. Allow your heart to show through. Exercise your emotions!

If we refuse to open up, to allow the full prism of His love and truth to shine through our lives, we will miss much of the color life has to offer.

> "I can't see, I can't see,"
>   says the man who won't look.

Are there colors in the rainbow?
   Are the meadows still green?
Are flowers still blooming,
   and butterflies seen?

"I can't hear, I can't hear,"
   says the man who won't listen.
Have birds stopped their singing?
   The brooks lost their song?
Has music stopped playing,
   the symphonies gone?

"I don't feel, I don't feel,"
   says the man who won't care.
Aren't feelings but knowing
   of good things and bad?
Of caring for others
   of gladness and sad?

"There's no life, there's no life,"
   says the man who won't live.
Life is naught but what is sought;
   yes, life is simply living.
And life is not collecting things,
   life is really giving.

"I'm not loved, I'm not loved,"
   says the man filled with rage.
Isn't love just reflections
   of what you first give
For all of the others,
   with whom you must live?

"There's no God, there's no God,"
   says the man with no faith.
See God's hand in the stars
   in the skies.
In the prayers of a child,
   in your silent sighs.

                   —Anonymous

9

Thinking Theologically About Sickness and Healing

OURS IS A WORLD OF enormous pain and hurt.

Every one of us knows someone who is enduring an intensely difficult time of physical or emotional trauma—or both.

We know sincere people of faith who have prayed for healing in their lives . . . and still they suffer.

We are also aware that there are those today who claim to have been healed instantaneously. They tell remarkable stories of miracles; they attended a meeting where an individual with certain "powers" touched them or simply spoke to them and . . . *whoosh!* . . . the Spirit healed them of their affliction.

Why are some healed, while many—*in fact, most*—are not? Why can some look back and claim a miracle while others must endure excruciating years of exhausting pain?

Some would prefer to overlook this, shrugging it off simply as "some have faith, others don't." Many of us cannot do that, however. We believe in the living God just as much as those who claim healing. We certainly want to serve His Son and uphold the work of the Spirit with equal sincerity and with passion. Yet we wonder how some could be relieved of an affliction almost overnight, while others must live with pain through lingering years of their lives. I know people right now in the church where I serve who wait for God to touch their lives and bring them back to a place of health they once knew. I also know people who were so sick they were rapping on death's door, yet only months later experienced healing and relief. All of this creates a dilemma within us. Needing to find answers to things that don't make sense, we are driven to do serious study on this subject as set forth in Scripture.

Because this dichotomy between sudden miraculous healings and an absence of miracles is such an important subject, and because of the high level of interest in healing and miracles today, I want to spend the next three chapters addressing this matter head-on in hopes of determining how all this relates—or does not relate—to the Spirit.

Dr. John White, in a book entitled *When the Spirit Comes with Power,* begins by describing several different and unusual events. One occurs in Malaysia, another one in Ohio, and yet another in Argentina. He describes these events rather carefully. Each falls into the category of phenomena—things that occurred which could not be explained in keeping with human logic. The question is: Were those things of the Spirit or were they not? Dr. White summarizes the stories with these words:

> Asia. North America. South America. These are three stories that I know about personally. I could also recount episodes from Africa and Europe. And there appear to be hundreds, if not thousands, of similar occurrences around the globe. What does it all mean? What are these reports of extreme emotional reactions and unusual behavior currently observed around the world among Christians of various theological persuasions—reports of great weeping or laughter, shaking, extreme terror, visions, falling (or what is sometimes called "being slain in the Spirit"), being "drunk with the Spirit" and other revival experiences? Something is certainly going on, and that something seems potent. Is it revival? Is it from God?
>
> We must be cautious in evaluating new religious movements. Many new movements are mediocre and a few, extremely dangerous. False fire burns fiercely, an angel of light still spreads his wings, and the elect continue to be deceived.
>
> Too often, however, we rely on rumor to determine what is going on. Sometimes our fear causes us to condemn

too quickly, especially concerning something new and spectacular. But is there a baby in the bath water? God himself has been known to act spectacularly so that there is always a danger of missing him in our skepticism. He is still at work in the world.[1]

We have already covered several intriguing subjects in this book on the Holy Spirit. I willingly and freely admit that I have not taken the "safe route." I have taken this risk because I, too, am unable to pass off many of these things with a shrug . . . or to simply claim that all the supernatural things I cannot explain are of the devil. Neither do I feel comfortable merely ignoring them. I have to think about them, and more often than not, I have to give answers that deal with that tough question: Why?

When issues like this arise, I must dig deeply into the Book of Truth to find reliable answers. And even then some of it remains vague, sometimes mysterious. Even one as gifted as Jonathan Edwards, the eighteenth-century intellectual and scholar who graduated from Yale (at age seventeen!) and became one of America's greatest philosophers and theologians, admitted this:

> And it has been very observable, that persons of the greatest understanding, and who had studied most about things of this nature, have been more confounded than others. Some such persons declare, that all their former wisdom is brought to nought, and that they appear to have been babes, who knew nothing.[2]

I confess to you, there are times I feel exactly like that! I will also freely admit that there are realms of this subject I do not know and probably never will know. And even after lengthy study, there are some things I simply can never explain with absolute certainty. But as we look at this together, hopefully some things regarding this matter of healing and miracles will become clearer. Yet I can assure you, some things will remain a mystery.

Before we begin, however, let me tell you why we must proceed with caution and why I want to be careful about what I write.

Second Corinthians 11 is a chapter written with passion by the apostle Paul to people he loved dearly and deeply. We can feel his passion simply by reading his words:

> For I am jealous for you with a godly jealousy; for I betrothed you to one husband, that to Christ I might present you as a pure virgin. But I am afraid, lest as the serpent deceived Eve by his craftiness, your minds should be led astray from the simplicity and purity of devotion to Christ.
>
> 2 Corinthians 11:2–3

Paul writes with the heart of a pastor, and I can certainly identify with that. Like Paul, I am intensely jealous for those whom I serve in ministry, for all those within the scope of our influence. Furthermore, his hope is my hope—to "present you as a pure virgin." I have had the privilege of leading some in our flock to Christ, introducing them to the joy of knowing God and walking with Him, and my heart is linked with them in their spiritual growth. But I agree with Paul: *I am afraid for many of them.* The thought of their being led astray greatly concerns me. I don't know of a pastor worth his salt who doesn't struggle with that same fear; namely, that his parishioners' "minds should be led astray from the simplicity and purity of devotion to Christ." Though I am not normally a worrier, I am more than slightly concerned over what people do with their pain, their brokenness, and especially their need for relief. Why? Because there are so many unbiblical and erroneous answers being offered which will only deceive, disillusion, disturb . . . and bring greater confusion.

Unfortunately, I have known individuals who have become so caught up in a pursuit of miracles that their devotion to Christ waned. My great hope is that this section of the book will keep that from happening in many lives.

Possible Sources of "Phenomenal Events"

I believe that miracles and healings—what we refer to as "phenomenal manifestations"—have four possible sources.[3]

First, *the manifestation could be self-induced.* This is another way of saying that the "miracle" or the "healing" could have a psychological explanation, in that it was either consciously or unconsciously self-induced.

For example, many people suffer from psychosomatic illnesses stemming from mental or emotional disturbances. When the mind or the emotions are healed, however, there is often a remarkable healing of the related physical ailment. Bodily pain or illnesses are erased simply by the removal of that which was troubling the individual.

Second, *the source of the manifestation could be highly charged, emotional meetings.* We could also call this category "mass hysteria" or "mass hypnosis." It is no secret that gifted speakers (especially preachers) can be extremely persuasive and accomplish amazing things with suggestible audiences. I have been in such meetings and watched it happen. In those situations the alleged "healing of the Spirit" is the result of brainwashing, mind-bending techniques employed by those who know how to move an audience.

Third: *The source could be satanic.* As we just read in 2 Corinthians 11, "the serpent deceived Eve." Paul's concern was that his friends in Corinth could have their minds led astray by the adversary's deceptive powers. Demonic forces love to ape the work of God. We must never forget that when Satan and his evil forces are involved in something, it is more often in the realm of light than in the realm of darkness!

Lucifer originally revealed himself as the angel of light, not the angel of darkness. He is not an ugly, grotesque creature with a red epidermis. On the surface he is an appealing, brilliant, persuasive, incredibly impressive being, as are his demons. He woos and wins people with logic and persuasive arguments and reasonable approaches. It looks right. It sounds good. It seems plausible. Yet it is still, at the core, satanic.

Even though the enemy of our souls may not prompt most phenomenal manifestations, no one can deny he is actively engaged in some.

Fourth, *the source could, in fact, be God*. Who could ever doubt God's power to heal? To deny that is to deny the Scriptures! He who creates life can certainly bring healing to it. Most evangelical Christians I know would not hesitate to say that the Lord heals. We have seen Him bring healing to fractured marriages, broken lives, and scarred emotions. Who of us would doubt then that He could heal physical and mental diseases? Why else do we pray for Him to intervene when we or someone we love gets sick?

I have a wonderful mental list of individuals whom I have known, prayed for, and stood with through times of great and threatening sicknesses. Today they are strong specimens of health. In many cases the attending physicians virtually gave up on them. I am convinced—and I assure you *they* are convinced—the Lord healed them. And so please do not close this book, toss it aside, and say with a sigh, "Swindoll does not believe that God heals." I do. I do with all my heart.

What I do not believe is that God has placed His healing powers in a few "anointed individuals" who claim to do divine healings. Nor do I believe that God is the source of all the proliferation of so-called healings today.

I realize that there are thousands of folks who sincerely believe it was the Lord who touched their lives and relieved their pain. My response is a cautious "perhaps He did . . . but maybe it wasn't God at all."

Foundational Facts Regarding Sin and Sickness

While I strongly advocate flying closer to the flame, I believe we must do so intelligently, cautiously, and wisely. Otherwise we can get burned. I know what I'm talking about having met and talked with many a "burn victim" in my years of pastoral ministry. It has been my observation that solid doses of sound theology could have prevented most of them from being consumed by error.

Those who search for reliable spiritual understanding must discipline themselves to think theologically. In the case of divine healing, we need to understand how God has put us together and how sin and sickness are interrelated. And as I examine the issues regarding sickness and healing, six facts seem essential to lay a solid theological foundation.

First: *Primarily, there are two types of sin—original and personal.*

Original sin is traced all the way back to the Garden of Eden, where Adam and Eve yielded to the temptation of the devil, fell into sin, and thereby lost their innocence. In their fall into sin, they introduced corruption—a spiritual pollution—that has permanently damaged humanity. This is called *Adamic sin*—or original sin—and it lies at the very core of our sin nature.

Ever since the Fall, it has been impossible to be born into this world without sin. We get it from our parents, who got it from theirs, who got it from theirs . . . all the way back to everyone's original parents, Adam and Eve. When Adam sinned, his act of disobedience polluted the stream of humanity, not unlike sewage waste pollutes a river.

> Therefore, just as through one man sin entered into the world, and death through sin, and so death spread to all men, because all sinned.
>
> Romans 5:12

Those words do not paint a very pretty picture, but the portrait is real nonetheless. The old hypothetical question: "If Adam and Eve had never sinned, would they have lived forever?" is answered easily: *Of course.* God's plan for them was a plan of innocence and perfection. His desire was that His created beings would walk with Him throughout their lives. His command, therefore, was that they not yield to the temptation to eat of the knowledge of the tree of good and evil.

And the LORD God commanded the man, saying, "From any
tree of the garden you may eat freely; but from the tree of the
knowledge of good and evil you shall not eat, for in the day
that you eat from it you shall surely die."

Genesis 2:16–17

Adam and Eve disobeyed, and the consequences were tragic.
Suffering, sickness, and death were introduced into the human
race, all stemming from sin. Had there never been sin, there
would never have been suffering or sickness or death. Remember
the words?

. . . and so death spread to all . . . because all sinned.

Romans 5:12b

Because all humans have this Adamic nature within, we com-
mit personal sins. Instead of obeying, we disobey. Instead of
choosing to walk with God, we resist Him, we run from Him, we
fight against Him. For,

all have sinned and fall short of the glory of God.

Romans 3:23

We are sinners by birth (original sin), and therefore we become sinners by choice (personal sin). In acting disobediently,
we bear the fruit of our Adamic root. Because deceit rests in our
nature, you and I deceive. Because disobedience rests in our
nature, we rebel. Because lawlessness is at our inner core, we act
it out in life.

I am not proud to admit it, but sometimes when a red light
stays red longer than I think it should, I impatiently run it. I am
not justifying my actions. On the contrary, I know in my mind I
should not run it. It is dangerous—and it is against the law. But
every once in a while I run a red light. Why? Because I am a rebel
by nature. And before you start feeling a little smug, let me remind you, *so are you!* Your rebellion may just take another form.

There is original sin and there are personal sins. Both result in serious consequences.

Second: *Original sin introduced sickness, suffering, and death to the human race.*

"The soul who sins will die."
Ezekiel 18:4

For since by a man came death, by a man also came the resurrection of the dead. For as in Adam all die, so also in Christ all shall be made alive.
1 Corinthians 15:21–22

"Man, who is born of woman,
Is short-lived and full of turmoil."
Job 14:1

No one is immune from sin and its consequences. As beautiful and lovely as your little girl, boy, or grandchild may be, that child was born with a sin nature. And that nature not only prompts disobedience, it is the source of sickness, suffering, and ultimately death. Those things are a part of the "fallout" of the Adamic nature. They are interwoven in all of humanity.

Third: *Often there exists a direct relationship between personal sins and physical sickness.*

At times, disobedience and rebellious acts are directly linked to some illness in the body.

Numerous examples of this are found in the Scriptures. Among the most notorious would be King David after his affair with Bathsheba.

As a result of his sinful behavior, David suffered grave physical and emotional consequences. The struggle he went through while hiding his adultery (including the murder of Bathsheba's husband) and living as a hypocrite and rebel led to such a crescendo of inner turmoil that David became physically ill. After Nathan confronted David and the king came to terms with his sin, he wrote a song of remembrance . . . his own painful testimony of those months of misery:

> When I kept silent about my sin, my body wasted
>   away
> Through my groaning all day long.
> For day and night Thy hand was heavy upon me;
> My vitality was drained away as with the fever-heat of
>   summer.
>   Psalm 32:3–4

David suffered intensely because he disobeyed God and then refused to face his sin. Guilt began eating away at him until it became so unbearable that he literally sighed and groaned as he was physically wasting away. He lost his appetite. He suffered from insomnia. He could not think clearly. He lost his energy. He suffered from a fever that wouldn't go away.

Imagine that kind of life. If you have ever been there, you don't need me to describe it. And while they may not have reached these proportions, most of us have known painful periods in our lives when we left our personal sins unaddressed and unconfessed. And the misery didn't leave until we dealt with our sin and disobedience. That is what happened to David:

> I acknowledged my sin to Thee,
> And my iniquity I did not hide;
> I said, "I will confess my transgressions to the LORD";
> And Thou didst forgive the guilt of my sin.
>   Psalm 32:5

What was it that made him sick? Guilt. What drained his energy? Guilt. What took away his happiness, his smile, his ability to think, his leadership skills? Guilt. There was a direct relationship between David's personal sins and the physical and emotional sickness that impacted his life.

Another example would be something Paul refers to in one of his letters to the Corinthians when he instructs them about their inappropriate behavior at the Lord's Table. Some, if you can believe it, used this as an occasion for gluttony and drunkenness. The apostle's words of reproof are powerful:

> For this reason many among you are weak and sick, and a number sleep.
>
> 1 Corinthians 11:30

In other words, their sin had resulted in weakness and sickness . . . and even in death!

Now remember, in such cases, the confession of sin begins the process of healing. The recovery may not be instantaneous (it usually isn't), but I have seen occasions when it has been. More often than not, however, the suffering begins to fade in intensity as the person experiences relief from guilt.

Fourth: *Sometimes there is no relationship between personal sins and human afflictions.*

This is a good time for me to caution you about being the messenger of God to every person who is ill, telling them, "There must be something wrong in your life." Occasionally you may be the appointed Nathan in some David's life. You may be the appointed one to say, "You are the man," or "You are the woman." But seldom do we have a right to say that. Because in many cases suffering or illness is not the result of personal sin.

A classic example of this would be the man who was born blind (referred to in John's Gospel). His congenital blindness had nothing to do with personal sins, either his own or his parents'.

> And as He passed by, He saw a man blind from birth. And His disciples asked Him, saying, "Rabbi, who sinned, this man or his parents, that he should be born blind?" Jesus answered, "It was neither that this man sinned, nor his parents; but it was in order that the works of God might be displayed in him.
>
> John 9:1–3

Jesus Himself states clearly that the man's physical affliction had nothing to do with personal sins.

Hebrews 4:14–15 also comes to mind.

> Since then we have a great high priest who has passed through the heavens, Jesus the Son of God, let us hold fast our confession. For we do not have a high priest who cannot sympathize with our weaknesses, but one who has been tempted in all things as we are, yet without sin.

If our weaknesses were always the result of sin, the writer would issue the command: "Confess your sins and you will be healed." But he says here, in effect, "Seeing us struggling with weaknesses, our Lord is moved over our affliction. He is touched with our struggles." He *doesn't* say, "Therefore, deal with the sin in your life and you will recover." On the contrary, His heart is moved over your pain. He grieves with you over the length of your depression. He sits alongside you in the hospital room as you live with the consequences of this dread malignancy . . . He is with you as you go through chemotherapy. He is touched with feelings of sympathy for you in your weaknesses.

Why? Because on these occasions there is no direct relationship between personal sins and sicknesses. Therefore, it is not a matter of confessing sins and claiming instant healing.

I have known people who have been gravely ill and have searched their heart to find whatever sin may have brought on their affliction. They confess and confess and confess. But their illness doesn't leave. Slowly, painfully, they waste away, wondering what they could have done that caused their sickness . . . when, in fact, their condition was not related to personal sin at all.

Fifth: *Sometimes it is not God's will that we be healed.*

Paul had the supernatural gift of healing that God gave the apostles. Yet he admits, "Trophimus I left sick at Miletus" (2 Tim. 4:20). Why was he "left sick"? Paul doesn't say, but if it were God's will that all be healed, that would not have occurred.

Then, in Philippians, we learn of a man named Epaphroditus who received God's mercy, even as his illness remained.

> Because he was longing for you all and was distressed because you had heard that he was sick. For indeed he was sick to the point of death, but God had mercy on him, and not on him only but also on me, lest I should have sorrow upon sorrow.
>
> Philippians 2:26–27

Here is a man who was sick—in fact, sick to the point of death—yet Paul, who had the gift of healing, was helpless to turn things around. Ultimately, God did have "mercy on him," but there was no instant turnaround in his condition.

Finally, consider Paul himself.

> And because of the surpassing greatness of the revelations, for this reason, to keep me from exalting myself, there was given me a thorn in the flesh.
>
> 2 Corinthians 12:7

The apostle suffered from a severe affliction—"a thorn in the flesh." The Greek term translated "thorn" means a sharp stake. Whatever it was, it brought piercing pain. Paul calls it a messenger of Satan (obviously allowed by God) to keep him genuinely humble.

Pain does that. You don't meet many arrogant people who are living with lingering pain. Pain buffets us. It breaks and humbles us.

And Paul says, "Concerning this." Concerning what? The thorn! The thorn!

> Concerning this I entreated the Lord three times that it might depart from me.
>
> 2 Corinthians 12:8

Time after time he pleaded for relief. When the pain reached the unbearable stage, this devoted servant of God begged God to take it away. Three times he made the same request: Heal me. Heal me. Heal me. Each time God's answer remained firm. No. No. No.

I repeat . . . sometimes it is not God's will that we be healed. Therefore, be very careful what you promise a person who is sick. If it were God's will for all people to be well, then there would be no sick people in the world. Or if it were the Lord's will to heal all those in His family, not one Christian would be ill.

Think biblically. Think theologically. If passages like this (and others) make a point clear, accept the truth, seek to understand it, and then apply it! God is there. Just because He chooses not to bring healing does not mean He has forsaken us. He is with us through the hardest time. His grace is still sufficient.

Sixth: *On some occasions it is God's will that we be healed.*

Since I plan to spend the next chapter dealing with this point, for now let's just take a quick glance at several verses in James 5.

> Is anyone among you suffering? Let him pray. Is anyone cheerful? Let him sing praises. Is anyone among you sick? Let him call for the elders of the church, and let them pray over him, anointing him with oil in the name of the Lord; and the prayer offered in faith will restore the one who is sick, and the Lord will raise him up, and if he has committed sins, they will be forgiven him.
>
> James 5:13–15

Yes, there are times when our Lord sovereignly chooses to "restore the one who is sick." This is His prerogative. As we shall see, when He miraculously intervenes, the healing is immediate, thorough, and permanent. And when that happens, He alone deserves the praise—never some human instrument.

I have heard it said that education is going from an unconscious to conscious awareness of one's ignorance. That statement applies to the Scriptures just as much as it does to life in general. Education in the Word of God awakens me to the vast realm of my ignorance. And I tend to back away and become less dogmatic about a lot of things once I become aware of this magnificent God whom I love and serve.

Flying closer to the flame does not remove all the mysteries contained in His will.

10

A Biblical Case for Healing

SOMETHING OCCURRED IN FEBRUARY 1975 that I will never forget. Cynthia and I, along with a number of alumni from Dallas Theological Seminary, were returning from the school's fiftieth anniversary celebration.

Back in those days they flew 747s between Dallas and the West Coast, and on this particular flight there were a number of empty seats in the large coach section. Our group was having a delightful time, reminiscing and laughing, telling stories from our student days. Perhaps it was our own high spirits that first made us notice the sad-looking couple several rows behind us. The woman was sitting near the aisle, but her husband was lying down, stretched out across four or five of the seats in the center section.

As we walked back and forth during the flight—getting something to drink or going to the bathroom—we made conversation with several passengers, including this couple. Both were friendly but extremely serious, and he did not look well. When the woman discovered that the people in our group were former classmates at a seminary and were now involved in various kinds of ministry, her interest in us heightened. And that's when she told us their story.

They were from Louisiana, she said, and her husband was deathly ill with cancer. They had been in touch with a famous "faith healer" on the West Coast (whom you would know if I named the person), and they had been promised that if they would come to Los Angeles and bring money, the so-called healer could guarantee her husband's relief from pain. When they returned to Louisiana, he would no longer have the cancer.

They were not "church people," as she put it, but they had watched this religious person on television. They had seen all the "wonders" and "healings" and "miracles" on television. By now, they were down to very few options. Together, they had agreed that this was what they should do.

The two of them were stacking all their hopes on that single promise, and to make certain they would have enough money, they sold everything they owned, including their home. They also had depleted their entire retirement savings. In fact, she showed me the bag of cash in her purse. (She mentioned that the contacts in the healing ministry had requested she bring cash.)

Through tears, she sighed, "I am willing to give up everything we own in order that my husband might be healed." Then she looked into my eyes, obviously longing for reassurance, and asked, "What do you think of such things?"

I'm sure you can appreciate the delicate and awkward silence that passed between us. My answer required tact mixed with honesty. Silently I prayed for just the right words. Then I opened my Bible and shared with her the things I believed. The woman listened carefully. Her husband tried to enter into our conversation, but he was obviously so ill that he was almost fading in and out of consciousness.

I mentioned my reservations and especially my concern regarding the depletion of all their savings. I restrained from unloading my strong convictions against paying someone for "doing a miracle." I did, however, try to explain my interpretation of what the Scriptures teach regarding healing versus healers.

She sighed and said, "I don't mean this the wrong way, but I hope you are wrong, because we have tried everything else. We believe God has led us to do this."

As we concluded our conversation, I said, "I'll tell you what: Here is my name, the address of the church I pastor in Fullerton, and my phone number." I also scribbled my home phone number on the little card I gave her. "Will you promise me that if your husband is healed, you will call me?"

With a smile she said, "Absolutely. I will call you, and you and I can celebrate."

I assured her, "I will truly celebrate with you," and then I prayed with the two of them shortly before our plane landed.

That was almost twenty years ago. I'm still waiting for her call.

Do I believe God can heal? With my whole heart! Do I believe God does heal? Absolutely. Have I seen cases where God has healed? Yes, I have, and I will mention a couple of them in this chapter.

Now the critical question: Do I believe God has placed His healing powers in a few "anointed individuals" who claim to do divine healings? I say, unequivocally, I do not. In fact, I don't think I have ever ministered to any more disillusioned souls than those who had been promised healing by an alleged "healer" and then were not healed.

In this day of the resurgence of so-called divine healers, my convictions may not represent a popular position. I realize that. In no way does this mean, however, that I do not believe God has the power to heal . . . and, on unique occasions, He does do so. I believe that with all my heart. The problem comes when attention is focused on a person who claims healing powers, or on the series of emotionally overpowering events that surround a so-called healing service. If those "divine healers" are authentic and "anointed" miracle workers of God, why aren't they out going floor-to-floor in hospitals and emergency wards? Why don't they prove the truth of their ministry there . . . humbly . . . unobtrusively . . . free of charge? Then I would have reason to believe they are servants of the living God in whose lives the Spirit is consistently pouring out His power to heal.

The all-powerful, living God certainly has the power to heal. However, in His inscrutable plan He has not removed all suffering, sickness, disease, and death from this world. I do not pretend to know why He sovereignly chooses to heal this one and not that one . . . a few and not all. But that is His choice; that is His right. I must minister to both. And ultimately, of course, even those who are healed at some point in their life must face the death of their earthly body. As someone has remarked, "We're all terminal!"

There are times when it is God's will that someone be healed, and when that is true, He does so miraculously and immediately. Be sure that you remember those two words, for they go together. When God is involved in the healing, it is both *immediate* and it is *miraculous*. Furthermore, it is free . . . as free as the gift of eternal life.

Remember when Peter and John happened upon the man crippled from birth who sat beside the temple begging? The man was hoping for a few shekels, but Peter said to him:

> "I do not possess silver and gold, but what I do have I give
> to you: In the name of Jesus Christ the Nazarene—walk!"
> Acts 3:6

And the man stood up and walked. Immediately! Miraculously! Freely! No one in that community had ever seen him walk before . . . yet he walked. And there is every reason to believe he remained permanently healed, for God's miraculous work in a person's life is *permanent*.

Back in the late 1950s I became close friends with a man who had been a fellow marine. Our friendship deepened as time passed, even though miles separated us. I was ministering in the state of Massachusetts, and he lived in Texas. Then one day I received a call from him.

"I need your prayers as I've never needed them before," he said in a rather grim voice. My immediate response was: "What is it?"

He said, "I have been diagnosed as having cancer of the tongue." Though he didn't cry easily, his voice broke as he continued. "I have been to the best medical specialists I can find here in the city of Dallas. They are all convinced it is cancer." He had also gotten a second opinion. And a third. They suggested he go to the Mayo Clinic in Rochester, Minnesota, so he and his wife were making the trip, carrying his x-rays with them. They were hoping, with the help of the doctors at the Mayo Clinic, he could at least come out of the surgery with a portion of his tongue.

"I'm asking you and about four other close friends to pray," he said. "Would you and Cynthia pray fervently for me?" He added, "I'm not announcing the need. I know that God can bring healing if it is His will, so let's pray for that. *Let's ask the Spirit of God to heal me!*" He assured me he had nothing sinful in his life that could have caused this to occur. "All I know is that the doctor says I have this malignant tumor. It is clearly evident in the x-rays. I just want you to pray that God, if it is His perfect will, will do a miracle." I assured him we would certainly pray with and for him.

As soon as I hung up the phone, I walked down the stairs to a little place in our basement where I would often go for quietness and prayer. Cynthia prayed with me for a while, then left to care for our children who were still small. I stayed for almost an hour, and as I prayed, God's "unidentified inner prompting" gave me an unusual sense of reassurance. I did not hear any voice. I did not see any vision. But I had an unusual feeling of confidence and a sense of peace about my friend's situation. I read several Scriptures, prayed for perhaps forty-five minutes, then I left it with God.

Two or three days later my phone rang again. I heard the voice of my friend on the other end of the line. By then he was in Minnesota, calling me from the Mayo Clinic.

"I have great news," he said.

I smiled to myself. "Well, what is it?"

"I have seen several specialists, and my wife and I have just met with our attending physician. He is baffled, Chuck. He tells us there is no cancer."

"Hey, this is great!" I replied. "Tell me what they said."

"Well," he responded, "actually they put me through all the tests again and took more x-rays. They don't believe I brought the correct x-rays with me, because the x-rays they took disagree so much with the ones I brought. I now have before me two sets of x-rays. One shows the cancer in the tongue as it was in Dallas. The other x-rays, taken here in Minnesota, are clear—no cancer." And with a touch of humor he continued, "So we had a remarkable flight from Dallas to Minnesota. Somehow, in some miraculous manner, the malignant tumor is nowhere to be found."

It was not only miraculous, it was also instantaneous, and it remained permanent. He never again had a problem with the pain or the growth in his tongue. My friend was a middle-aged man and had many wonderful years in front of him, which he lived to the fullest. His subsequent death—many years later—was brought on by an unrelated disease.

I can't explain what happened. He couldn't either. I have no powers within me that produce healing in anyone else. The God I know is the same God you know, and I simply trusted Him and prayed for His will to be done. The Spirit of God healed my friend sovereignly and silently. And best of all, God got all the glory.

Following the Steps Prescribed in Scripture

I find it curious that most folks take their cues from televangelists and other religious public figures rather than the Bible when it comes to seeking divine healing. I find it even more curious in light of the sideshow tactics of these performers. I remember seeing—on one of the rare occasions when I've tuned in—one rather popular individual sling his suit coat against the sick and the crippled and blow his breath on them. While his audience screamed and applauded, I flinched and grieved, thinking, *What kind of a show is this?* As I watched one person after another suddenly keel over, I wondered, *Who originated the strange idea that that's what it means to be "slain in the Spirit"?*

But what I really wonder is why folks don't follow the prescribed steps spelled out in the Scriptures instead of joining in the theatrics of the media circus? Without meaning to sound harsh, who canceled out the inspired guidelines and substituted the current script and style? I'm serious. Why do so many evangelical Christians adopt all the fleshly pizazz and ignore the simple one-two-three process described in the New Testament? Could it be they just don't know? Perhaps.

I'm referring to the instructions set forth in James 5:13–16. If you have never given serious thought to these words, and if you sincerely wish to pursue the Spirit's healing work in your life, please read the rest of this chapter slowly and carefully. Set aside all the other stuff you have heard and witnessed on television . . . and focus your full attention on God's inspired instructions.

> Is anyone among you suffering? Let him pray. Is anyone cheerful? Let him sing praises. Is anyone among you sick? Let him call for the elders of the church, and let them pray over him, anointing him with oil in the name of the Lord; and the prayer offered in faith will restore the one who is sick, and the Lord will raise him up, and if he has committed sins, they will be forgiven him. Therefore, confess your sins to one another, and pray for one another, so that you may be healed. The effective prayer of a righteous man can accomplish much.
>
> James 5:13–16

Those Who Are "Suffering"

Clearly, James sets forth three categories of people in the church. First, there are those whom he identifies simply as suffering—"Is anyone among you suffering?" There is nothing more said to the "suffering" than, "Let him pray."

Intrigued by the term *suffering*, I did a quick search on the Greek term *kakopatheia* and discovered it is used in this form only here in the New Testament. Actually it is used in one other form only three times, and on those occasions it is found in 2 Timothy, Paul's last letter. Each of the three times Paul uses it, it is translated "suffer hardship." I found that the word means "to be the brunt of mistreatment, to be suffering from persecution, from misunderstanding, to be suffering from hard times or difficult times." The original word does not refer to a physical disease.

Our friends who lost their homes in the terrible rains and fires and earthquakes out here in California went through *kakopatheia* . . . hard times. Individuals who are experiencing persecution at work because of their faith are enduring *kakopatheia*. They are going through hardship. Those going through such times are instructed to pray. That's it. They are not promised anything special—not even assured that the pain will pass or that the suffering will stop. But in the praying, new strength comes to the petitioner, strength to endure, the ability to withstand hardship. So when such external difficulties occur, the very best answer is to pray . . . tap into the source of invincible power!

Those Who Are "Cheerful"

The second category is the antithesis of suffering: "Is anyone cheerful?" Happily, there are always a few who are cheerful. What are they to do? "Let him sing praises!" We are instructed not to hold back our praise.

I get so weary of somber Christians who look like they have been baptized in lemon juice—like it's borderline carnal to laugh and have a great time, to sing heartily and enjoy the overflowing blessings of God.

I have spent some time with Christians who have been blessed with prosperity. When we are together they are cheerful and full of praise. But they often say that they haven't the freedom to express their joy openly. "We don't dare let anybody know that it has been a marvelous year for us. We don't let the word out that our business is doing great." Such prosperity is considered taboo in many Christian circles. Nonsense! When the Lord blesses someone else abundantly, we should rejoice with him or her without feeling that He must bless us in the same way before we can do so. May the Lord give us such maturity and grace.

Being cheerful is not limited to those who are prosperous. I have known cheerful Christians in every walk and circumstance of life. To all who are cheerful, regardless of anything external, James says, "Let him sing praises." Let the joyful times roll!

Those Who Are "Sick"

This third category is the one we will focus on for the balance of this chapter: "Is anyone among you sick?" The term translated "sick" is the Greek word *astheneo,* which means "to be weak, to be without strength." It suggests even "to be disabled, to be incapacitated." This is talking about a serious illness, not merely a headache or chronic backache or twenty-four-hour flu.

The man we met on the airplane back in 1975 would qualify. He was so sick they had to transport him off the plane in a wheelchair. He was *astheneo.*

Now let's walk, step-by-step, through the procedure described here in James 5. Remember, this is based on inspired instructions from the Spirit of God as He moved upon James to write these things.

First, *the sick person takes the initiative.*

Is anyone among you sick? Let him [let the sick one] call for the elders of the church . . .

James 5:13

Often the elders and other church leaders are the last to know when someone is sick. Sometimes parishioners who are ill feel neglected and even think that pastors and elders really don't care when, in fact, they have never been told!

Let me make it very clear: There is no massive crystal ball in a pastor's study. There is no all-knowing computer that reads out all the names of the congregation on a daily basis and puts those who are feeling bad in flashing lights. I don't mean to make light of this. My point is that the only way for pastors or elders to know anyone is seriously ill is for someone to communicate that need.

Second, *when the elders arrive, they carry out two functions.* Before describing those dual functions, let me point out a particular construction in the original Greek sentence that will help clarify this part of the healing procedure. It is found in verse 14, which reads, *literally:*

> Is anyone among you sick? Let him call for the elders of the church, and let them pray over him, *having anointed him with oil* in the name of the Lord [emphasis mine].

Yes, the instructions are to be followed in the correct order: "let them pray over him, having anointed him with oil." The anointing with oil, therefore, would *precede* the time spent in prayer. Stay with me. As you see the passage unfold, you will understand the significance of this.

There are two Greek words for "anoint." One always has a religious and ceremonial connotation; the other, a practical one. David's head was anointed with oil before he came to the throne of Israel . . . a ceremonial anointing, acknowledging that he was the king-elect. However, you would never tell someone that you "anointed" your bike with oil because it was squeaking . . . or that you "anointed" your sewing machine with oil. Such a procedure is practical. It has no religious connotation at all. Now, of the two words, it is the latter that is used here, the practical one. "Anointing," therefore, is not really a good rendering of the original term. "Rubbing" would be a better translation.

When the Good Samaritan stopped and took care of the man who had been beaten along the road to Jericho, he poured oil and wine into the man's wounds. He "rubbed" those ingredients into the man's wounds. The same term appears in ancient Greek medical treatises where oil was prescribed for the purpose of medication. All of this may seem like needless and tedious detail, but in fact these things are basic to an accurate understanding of God's inspired instructions.

"Anoint" here refers to the practical application of proper medicine, or, in today's terms, to the appropriate professional help as well as prescribed medication. In other words, "See your doctor and follow his instructions." That comes first. *Then,* after appropriate medical attention, there is to be prayer.

I'll tell you how strongly I believe in following this process. I find it very hard to pray for someone who refuses to consult a doctor and follow his or her orders . . . or who refuses to take the medication that is prescribed . . . or who refuses the therapy recommended. Unlike the so-called divine healers, I believe it is biblical for those who are seriously ill not only to seek medical attention, but to do that *first.*

Those seeking miracles, first and foremost, often consider the consulting of a physician as an unwillingness to trust God. Such an extremist position is not only unwise, it is unbiblical. Back in ancient days, because there were so few medical doctors, it fell upon the elders to apply appropriate medication, such as oil applied to the body, or whatever may have been necessary. Medical assistance is not an enemy of the healing process.

A man I have admired from a distance is Dr. C. Everett Koop, the former United States surgeon general. In a book entitled *The Agony of Deceit,* Dr. Koop writes the chapter, "Faith-Healing and the Sovereignty of God." He begins by declaring:

> I don't know how many operations I actually performed in my surgical career. I know I performed 17,000 of one particular type, 7,000 of another. I practiced surgery for thirty-nine years, so perhaps I performed at least 50,000 operations.[1]

That gives you some idea of his enormous experience in the disciplines of medicine. He continues:

> A surprising number of Christians are convinced God will not be believed unless He makes tumors disappear, causes asthma to go away, and pops eyes into empty sockets. But the gospel is accepted by God-given faith, not by the guarantee that you will never be sick, or, if you are, that you

will be miraculously healed. God is the Lord of healing, of growing, of weather, of transportation, and of every other process. Yet people don't expect vegetables without plowing. They don't expect levitation instead of getting in a car and turning a key—even for extraordinarily good and exceptional reasons.

Although God *could* do all of this, Christian airline pilots do not fly straight into a thunderstorm after asking God for a safe corridor, although He could give them such safety. We do not have public services and ask God to remove all criminals, prostitutes, and pornographers from our midst, although He *could* do that too. God could eliminate AIDS from our planet. While we pray for a speedy discovery of successful treatment, I must do all I can to employ medical science in its task, as all health care professionals must do.[2]

In my opinion, not enough is said from evangelical pulpits regarding those who serve the sick in the field of medicine—physicians, nurses, therapists, you name it. What a fine and necessary body of caring people. But they are not miracle workers. They do not pretend to be. But they have received careful training and therefore have wisdom and understanding needed by those who are sick. And many of them who are Christians have a quiet, sincere appreciation for the presence of God in the midst of their profession. While there may be a few who are unqualified and uncaring, they do not represent the majority in the medical field. If our Lord cared enough about medication to mention it in a passage such as this, it certainly should be honored and applied in our age of advanced technology.

In the process of finding relief from sickness, medical assistant and proper medication play an important role. Remember, however, following the oil, they were to pray. Being men of faith, genuinely committed to God's will being carried out, the elders would have prayed fervently, believingly, offering up strong, confident, and yet humble prayers of intercession.

Third: *Specific results are left in the Lord's hands.* His will was sought, not the empty promises of some earthly individual.

> . . . let them pray over him, anointing him with oil *in the name of the Lord* [emphasis mine].

Don't overlook those last few words. Doing something "in the name of the Lord" was a colloquialism in that day for "the will of God." Today we might say, "Have them apply the oil, then pray for the will of God." And the result?

> . . . and the prayer offered in faith will restore the one who is sick.

Be careful not to yank that statement out of its context and quote it alone. Verses 14 and 15 are inseparably woven together in the same piece of biblical tapestry. The elders are praying over this person in the name of the Lord—that is, invoking God's will, asking God's presence, God's blessing—and the result? Actually, it's in God's hands. When it is His sovereign will to bring healing, it will occur. And in that case, "the prayer offered in faith will restore the one."

The Greek word here translated "restore" is *sozo*. It means "to save." So the prayer offered in faith will literally save the sick person's life. Why? Because in that case it is God's will for healing to occur.

> . . . and the Lord will raise him up, and if he has committed sins, they will be forgiven him.

There is another important term here: "The Lord *will raise* him up." This looks miraculous to me . . . a case of instantaneous healing. And don't overlook the additional comment: "if he has committed sins, they will be forgiven him."

Perhaps the person's past was marked by sins—extended, serious sins. If this is the root of the problem, there will be an admission of it in the process of the healing. Remember the third "foundational fact" in the previous chapter? There is often a direct relationship between personal sins and physical sickness.

This reminds me of an experience I had many years ago when I was ministering at a church in another city. The person who was seriously ill was a believer who happened to be the wife of a medical doctor. She suffered from terrible, almost unbearable pain all across her back. Physicians could not find the cause. Several competent orthopedic specialists worked together on her case, all to no avail. Then they wondered, could the pain be the result of some psychological struggle? A psychiatrist was consulted; still no relief. She sought neurological counsel as well. Perhaps the problem was centered in the spine, the nervous system. Again they were unable to find the answer.

Her incredible pain had led the physicians to begin intense medication that could become habit forming, and her husband was very concerned about that, naturally, as was she. Finally, they hospitalized the woman.

Because we were longtime friends, she contacted me and asked, "I wonder, Chuck, if you could get together a group of the elders from the church and if several of you could come and pray?" I responded, "Certainly we'll come." And we went, about six or seven of us.

We walked into her hospital room on a Sunday night following the evening service. She was in such pain she could hardly talk. "I don't know what I'm going to do," she said. "I'm getting desperate." Her husband was on call that night, so he was not there when we arrived; he came in later as we were praying. I talked with her briefly about the medication and the assistance she was getting. She had no complaints. She felt everyone was doing all they could do. She asked, "What can *we* do? What can we *do?*" I replied, "We can do what God instructed us to do . . . *pray*. We will pray that if it is His sovereign will, He will save you, restore you, raise you up!"

We closed the door, turned the lights down, and several of us dropped to our knees and began to pray. I finished my prayer by pleading with God to bring relief and, if it were His will, to bring full restoration. As another man began to pray, the woman reached down and touched me on the shoulder. She was pushing on me, as if she wanted to say something. I reached over to the man who was praying and took him by the knee and held tightly, as if to say, "Wait a minute." He stopped. Spontaneously, she said, "Excuse me for interrupting, but the pain is all gone." And she began to weep. Several of us wept as well. We were so grateful to God at that moment.

"I must tell all of you something," the woman said, and she sat up in bed—something she had not been able to do for days. Actually I think she could have gotten up and walked out of the hospital, stepped into her car, and driven home that night. The pain was completely gone. She said, "I need to tell you something about my life." Quietly, yet without hesitation, she began to unfold a story of sin that had been a part of her lifestyle. It is not necessary that I go into the details . . . only to say that she had been living a life of deception before us as well as before her family. But there had been something compelling about our prayer and the sincerity of our faith gathered around her that brought her to such a burning awareness of her sin she couldn't even let us finish. God heard her prayer of confession and desire for repentance.

Let's not miss verse 16:

> Therefore, confess your sins to one another, and pray for one another, so that you may be healed. The effective prayer of a righteous man can accomplish much.

This does not refer to a general public acknowledgment before the whole church of every dirty, lustful thought you have had in the last week. That is not the context. The verse refers to a person who is ill and who knows that he or she is living a lifestyle that is wrong and therefore needs to bring that out into the open, to confess it to those who are spiritually concerned and praying for him or her. The result? Cleansing within . . . healing without.

My friend was released from the hospital the next day; she never returned. In less than a week, she was jogging, enjoying full, pain-free health. And to my knowledge she never had the pain again. She wrote me on two occasions to thank me again and again, though I deserved no thanks. All I did—along with a group of like-minded men—was do what God's Word instructed and counted on God to do His will. And in that case, it was to raise her up . . . miraculously and instantaneously.

As a small group of individuals who had no "healing gifts" prayed and asked God to intervene, He did. It was God who did the healing. When we discovered that the proper "oil" had been applied, there was nothing left to do but get as close to the flame as possible . . . and *pray*.

Four Practical Principles to Claim

As we carefully work our way through these instructive verses, several timeless principles emerge, all of which are worth claiming today.

1. *Confession of sin is healthy—employ it.* When you find that you are wrong, say it. When you have done something offensive to another person, admit it. Confess it to God and then find the person you have hurt and confess it to that person. Full confession can lead to full restoration.

2. *Praying for one another is essential—practice it.* When someone says, "Will you pray for me?" take the request to heart. Don't just glibly respond, "Oh, yeah, sure," then promptly forget about it. Ask for some details. Write down the specific requests. I have a little notepad on my desk in my study, and when someone requests prayer, I write down the person's name and needs. I won't remember if I don't write it down. Later on, I like to follow up and ask if God has answered prayer.

3. *Medical assistance is imperative—obey it.* Regardless of the ailment, the nature of the illness, or the excuses you may be tempted to use to cut that corner, seeking medical assistance is

both wise and helpful. And when the physician prescribes or suggests—obey!

4. *When healing comes from God—claim it.* Praise Him for it. Don't give credit for your healing to some person on this earth. God alone is responsible for your relief. Healing doesn't come because you pay someone for it or stand in line for it or appear before some individual who claims he or she is able to do it. Healing comes because God sovereignly and mysteriously chooses to say yes to you. It falls under the heading of undeserved favor—GRACE.

I close by quoting Dr. Everett Koop once again:

> The faith healer may say that faith makes God act. If you follow that line of reasoning, God is in His heaven, but Bosworth rules the world! In Matthew 8:2–3, where Jesus heals a leper, we read:
>
> > Behold, a leper came and worshiped Him, saying, "Lord, if You are willing, You can make me clean." Then Jesus put out His hand and touched him, saying, "I am willing; be cleansed." And the leper departed. *And slowly, over the course of the next several weeks, his symptoms began to disappear.*
>
> I am sure you realize that this is not what the Bible says. I put it in those terms because that conforms to a lot of "miraculous healings" today. The healing takes place next month. But what the Word of God says is this: "'I am willing; be cleansed.' And *immediately* his leprosy was cleansed" (NKJV, italics added).
>
> Now I know that all healing comes from God, but if we are to pursue this matter of faith healing so that I do not have any questions, this is what I want to see: I want to see a person with one leg suddenly ("immediately") have two. In fact, I want to see a person cold, flat-out dead, get up and walk. Now it is not that I want to see these miracles take place just to satisfy my own curiosity. I want to see them happen in such a way that there is no praise attributed to the faith healer. And I want to see it done in a situation that is not a

carnival. Now if all of those conditions were in place, I suspect that a healing service would occur very much in private. . . .

Giving that great Reformed theologian from Princeton, B. B. Warfield, credit for his contribution to my thinking on this subject, let me summarize in the following way. There is no promise anywhere in the Scriptures of miraculous healing for those who will claim it. Anywhere. No facts exist that compel us to believe that such miraculous healing should be expected. Such *miraculous* healing is unnecessary, because God is perfectly capable of healing people by natural means. The employment of such a method is contrary to the way God works in other modes of dealing with us. Miraculous healings of the type I have been describing would be contrary to the very purpose of "miracle." If miracles were commonplace, they would soon lose their significance.[3]

Yes, God does heal. And when He does, it is miraculous . . . immediate . . . permanent . . . and free. It's all in His hands. But don't look for healings around every corner. God's not in the sideshow business. After all, "if miracles were commonplace, they would soon lose their significance."

11

When the Spirit Brings a Slow Recovery

*H*IPPOCRATES WAS A GREEK physician considered by many to be "the Father of Medicine." It was he who wrote the Hippocratic Oath taken by all those entering the practice of medicine. He lived about 450 to 375 B.C., which made him a contemporary of such philosophers as Socrates, Dionysius, Plato, and Aristotle. Hippocrates wrote much more than the famous oath that bears his name, and most of his writings, as we might expect, have to do with human anatomy, medicine, and healing.

In a piece entitled *Aphorisms,* for example, he wrote: "Extreme remedies are very appropriate for extreme diseases." In *Precepts,* these words appear in the first chapter: "Healing is a matter of time." While reading those pieces of human wisdom recently, it occurred to me that one might connect them in a paraphrase that would have a rather significant and relevant ring to it: "Recovering from extreme difficulties usually requires an extreme amount of time."

In our world of "instant" everything, that may not sound very encouraging. Yet it is, more often than not, true. The deeper the wound, the more extensive the damage, the greater amount of time is needed for recovery. Wise counsel, Hippocrates! We tend to forget your insightful advice.

Where would the old Greek get such wisdom? His *Aphorisms* and *Precepts* sound almost like the Proverbs of Solomon. As a matter of fact, his writings sound a bit like Solomon.

While entertaining that thought the other day, I pondered an idea I had never considered before. Hippocrates lived sometime between Solomon the king and Paul the apostle—what is known in biblical history as the between-the-Testaments era, that four-hundred-year span when no Scripture was being written, although the Old Testament books were being compiled. So could it be that the Greek physician-philosopher, in his research, came across some of Solomon's writings and rephrased a line or two? For example, isn't it possible that something from Solomon's journal (Ecclesiastes, by name) could have found its way into Hippocrates' writings? Consider the first few lines from Ecclesiastes 3:

> There is an appointed time for everything. And there is a time
> for every event under heaven—
> > A time to give birth, and a time to die;
> > A time to plant, and a time to uproot what is planted.
> > A time to kill, and a time to heal;
> > A time to tear down, and a time to build up.
> > > Ecclesiastes 3:1–3

Tucked away in that third verse is the phrase that intrigues me, "a time to heal." Perhaps I am only imagining all this, but I cannot help but wonder if Hippocrates' words, "Healing is a matter of time," might have found their origin in Solomon's statement. In any event, the statement remains sound, both medically and biblically. Except in cases of God's miraculous intervention, healing takes time. And, I repeat, the greater the disease or damage, the longer it takes to heal.

I have been concerned about this issue for a long, long time. Throughout my years in ministry I have had a great deal of contact with people who hurt. In every church I've pastored, in every community in which I've lived, anguish and affliction have abounded. And the pain has come from every conceivable source.

Those who have seemed most disillusioned, however, have been the ones who prayed for but did not experience a quick recovery. Many of them were promised such by people who held out the hope of a miracle. When the anticipated divine intervention did not transpire, their anguish reached the breaking point. I have looked into their faces and heard their cries. I have witnessed their response—everything from quiet disappointment to bitter, cursing cynicism . . . from tearful sadness to violent acts of suicide. And most have been sincere, intelligent, Christian people.

Even though I would love to perform instant miracles for those who need healing (or at least promise recovery "within a week or two"), I am not able to do so. Maybe that is the reason I am so intrigued with the combined thoughts of Hippocrates and Solomon. Since I deal constantly with people in pain, I am left to search for answers that make sense, even though they will never make headlines.

This chapter is about the answers I have found. I have no cure-all solutions to offer, no secret formula that will have you on your feet, smiling, in twenty-four hours. I wish I did, but I don't. I do have some things to say, however, that may give you fresh hope and renewed perspective in the recovery process.

Everything I have to say finds it origin in Scripture, God's unfailing, ever-reliable Book of Truth. If you are weary of the sensational, if the get-well-quick answers haven't worked for you, if it seems that the miracles of overnight relief are for someone else, then perhaps this chapter is especially for you. If your healing is taking a long time, I hope you will find comfort in these pages. And the plain fact is this: For most folks, healing is a slow, arduous process. It takes time.

Time to Heal

I have seen a lot of bumper stickers that read: I'D RATHER BE SAILING. But I have never seen one that read: I'D RATHER BE SHIPWRECKED! I doubt I ever will. Sailing across the water is an exhilarating experience, but sinking under the water is nothing short of terrifying, especially if the sea is rough and the winds are stormy.

Having spent over a month on the ocean during my days in the Marine Corps, I have had my share of high waves and maddening windstorms. On one occasion the swells were somewhere between thirty and forty feet high, and no one—not even the skipper (we found out later!)—thought we would ever see land again. Talk about feeling helpless! Going through such life-threatening situations gives one an absolutely realistic perspective on and respect for the sea. I never see a large ocean-going vessel without having a flashback to my days on the Pacific. How different from what I expected! Instead of an uninterrupted calm, relaxed voyage in the buoyant waters of the deep, my whole world was turned topsy-turvy. Every time I hear some novice speak glibly about how much fun it would be to sail a little boat across the seas, I shudder inside. What we expect is seldom what we experience.

This came home to me in a fresh way some time ago when I read about the twenty-year reunion of most of those who were involved in the formation of the old American Football League. The seasoned sports veterans and owners swapped stories and enjoyed an evening of laugher and reflections together. Among those present was Al Davis, currently the owner of the Los Angeles Raiders, who remembered that all those sitting at his table had stared with envy at Nicky Hilton, who was to speak on that eventful evening in 1959 when they first met to form the league. Everyone's feelings of expectation were only heightened when the man was introduced as having recently made $100,000 in the baseball business in the city of Los Angeles.

Mr. Hilton stood to his feet as the place broke into thunderous applause. Then he stepped to the microphone and said he needed to correct what had been said. It was not he who had had that experience; it was his brother Baron. And it wasn't in Los Angeles, but San Diego. And it wasn't baseball, it was football. And it wasn't $100,000, it was $1 million . . . and he didn't make it, he *lost* it!

Realism always takes the wind out of idealism's sails!

Historical Interruption

That's exactly what happened to Paul, who lived during the first century. For years he had one great dream: to go to Rome, the capital of the empire. The driving force of his life was to have an audience with the Caesar (Nero) and, eyeball-to-eyeball, present to him the claims of Jesus Christ.

A Dream Becomes a Nightmare

Not a bad idea! Sounds like a worthy objective . . . and when you consider that getting there called for a lengthy trip aboard ship from Palestine to Italy, you could almost envision a Mediterranean cruise to boot. But it wasn't a cruise (as we saw in chapter 7); it was a disaster. The ship didn't sail; it sank. And he didn't arrive immediately in Italy; he landed fifty miles out of Sicily. And it wasn't the splendid metropolis of Rome; it was the rugged island named Malta.

That's the bad news! The good news is that "they all were brought safely to land" (Acts 27:44).

All 276 swam, gagged, gasped, struggled, and finally sloshed ashore, soaked and exhausted . . . but safe. It was an unexpected, tumultuous, distant detour.

That's how it is when you find yourself dumped on an island named Malta when all along you had Italy in your sights and the dream of Rome in your heart.

The Beginning of Recovery

Allow me, however, to add a practical dimension to this story that is easily overlooked. Sometimes we sailors on the sea of life need what places like Malta can provide. It may seem to be a barren, lonely, desperate spot, but its solitude is therapeutic, and in its quiet, gentle breezes are renewal, refreshment, and healing. In a word, I'm referring to full recovery from some longstanding struggle, which, I remind you, takes time.

May I go deeper? God plans our Maltas. These transitional islands may seem forlorn and fearsome, especially if you arrive there on the ship of despair, suffering from a neurotic drive to accomplish more, more, more. Those who opt for burning out en route to Rome fear rusting out at Malta, but that doesn't occur. On the contrary, it takes Malta to show us how to stop just existing and start living again. What appears as nothing more than the death of a dream is, in actuality, the first step in the process of healing.

As any student of the New Testament would tell you, Paul's life over the previous twelve to fifteen months had been anything but serene. He had appeared before several frowning judges in one courtroom scene after another. He had experienced mob violence, physical abuse, demonic and satanic oppression, imprisonment, the pain of misunderstanding by friend and foe alike, and more than one threat on his life. Most of those things he endured alone . . . so toss in the loneliness factor. The storm at sea was a fitting and climactic analogy for those long months prior to the voyage to Rome. Forgive me if I sound uncaring, but it took a shipwreck to jolt Paul's perspective back into focus. The disaster at sea followed by the forced change of pace on Malta was precisely what he needed for the process of recuperation and repair to begin.

Sir Winston Churchill, prime minister of England during the 1940s and 1950s, was a leader I have admired for many years. Through intense years of political pressure, heightened by his country's devastating war with Nazi Germany, Churchill maintained a remarkable sense of balance. His wisdom and wit remained intact, and panic never seemed to drain his inner reservoir of confident hope. He once wrote a brief essay entitled "Painting As a Pastime" in which he unveiled his secret of sustaining such a peaceful mind-set.

> Many remedies are suggested for the avoidance of worry and mental overstrain by persons who, over prolonged periods, have to bear exceptional responsibilities and discharge

duties upon a very large scale. Some advise exercise, and others, repose. Some counsel travel, and others retreat. Some praise solitude, and others, gaiety. No doubt all these may play their part according to the individual temperament. But the element which is constant and common in all of them is Change.

Change is the master key. A man can wear out a particular part of his mind by continually using it and tiring it, just in the same way as he can wear out the elbows of his coat. There is, however, this difference between the living cells of the brain and inanimate articles: one cannot mend the frayed elbows of a coat by rubbing the sleeves or shoulders; but the tired parts of the mind can be rested and strengthened, not merely by rest, but by using other parts. It is not enough merely to switch off the lights which play upon the main and ordinary field of interest; a new field of interest must be illuminated. It is no use saying to the tired mental muscles—if one may coin such an expression—"I will give you a good rest." "I will go for a long walk," or "I will lie down and think of nothing." The mind keeps busy just the same. If it has been weighing and measuring, it goes on worrying. It is only when new cells are called into activity, when new stars become the lords of the ascendant, that relief, repose, refreshment are afforded.

A gifted American psychologist has said, "Worry is a spasm of the emotion; the mind catches hold of something and will not let it go." It is useless to argue with the mind in this condition. The stronger the will, the more futile the task. One can only gently insinuate something else into its convulsive grasp. And if this something else is rightly chosen, if it is really attended by the illumination of another field of interest, gradually, and often quite swiftly, the old undue grip relaxes and the process of recuperation and repair begins.[1]

Lest you think that "doing nothing" is all that is involved in one's stopover at Malta, Churchill's counsel has been mentioned here. Paul does not merely walk along the beach and finger a few seashells . . . nor does he spend weeks staring at sunsets, wiggling his toes in the sand. For him to heal, change was needed, not simply stoic silence.

Personal Treatment

Dr. Luke, the writer of the Acts narrative, mentions a couple of the incidents that transpired between Paul and the island natives. The New English Bible refers to these people as "rough island-ers," implying that they had limited education and were driven by superstitious beliefs, which is seen in the account we're about to examine.

Extraordinary Kindness

Initially, the shipwreck victims were greeted with extraordinary kindness. An early-winter rainstorm drenched the island and left everyone shivering because of the cold. Unusually hospitable, the islanders built a large fire and treated the visitors with a marked degree of kindness.

Suddenly, however, the scene changes.

> And the natives showed us extraordinary kindness; for because of the rain that had set in and because of the cold, they kindled a fire and received us all. But when Paul had gathered a bundle of sticks and laid them on the fire, a viper came out because of the heat, and fastened on his hand. And when the natives saw the creature hanging from his hand, they began saying to one another, "Undoubtedly this man is a murderer, and though he has been saved from the sea, justice has not allowed him to live."
>
> Acts 28:2–4

Unjust Criticism

Aroused and angered by the fire, a viper crawled out of the stack of timber and attached itself to Paul's hand. The snake's bite was so deep and penetrating that Paul was unable to shake his hand free. When the natives witnessed this, they jumped to a conclusion that was both cruel and inaccurate: They were suddenly convinced that Paul's calamity was proof that he was guilty of some crime.

Interestingly, even though these barbarians (the actual Greek term here that is translated "natives") lacked education and refined culture, they had an inner standard of justice. Their opinion, however incorrect, was an instantaneous one: "Undoubtedly this man is a murderer." To them the snakebite represented justice having her due.

There is something amazingly relevant about this episode. A "punishment" mind-set is not limited to rough islanders in the Mediterranean. Heathen tribespeople aren't the only ones who jump to the erroneous conclusion that those who suffer are simply "getting what they deserve." Justified punishment—"calamity is proof of guilt." Abominable theology!

I wish there were some way for sufferers to be delivered from such unjust and unfair criticism. It is painful enough to endure the severe blows of life . . . but when words of condemnation coming from superstition and prejudice bite into us, causing the venom of guilt to spread and poison our minds, it is almost more than we can bear.

Inappropriate Exaltation

Quickly, however, Paul shook off the viper. As it fell into the fire, leaving him free from any ill effects, the natives' eyes grew large with amazement. They waited and waited for Paul to drop dead. When he didn't, when they witnessed his resilience, "they changed their minds and began to say that he was a god."

I cannot help but smile when I read this abrupt change of opinion. First, the man is a murderer; now he's a god. When calamity struck, he was getting his due—punishment by death. But once he recovered, he was suddenly catapulted to the superhuman realm, and they were ready to worship him.

A. T. Robertson, a New Testament scholar of yesteryear, points out Paul's similar experience in reverse many years before this encounter on Malta. That one occurred in Lystra, where Paul was first elevated to the place of a god, Mercury, only to be stoned shortly thereafter by the very same people who had earlier deified him. With seasoned wisdom, Dr. Robertson adds this biting comment, "So fickle is popular favor."[2]

It is quite possible that your situation today has been intensified by a similar reversal of opinion. You once knew success. You had the respect of others. You were in demand: a competent, admired, highly honored individual who drank daily from the well of fresh praise . . . right? How things have changed! You now find yourself "shelved" and virtually passed by, perhaps even hated by a few. Your world has suffered a head-on collision, and you're bloody from having gone through the windshield of reversed reputation. Those who once quoted you now criticize you. "So fickle is popular favor."

If that is the case, let me remind you . . . full recovery calls for a *healing that will take time*. And it cannot occur, unfortunately, without some scars remaining. The two scars you will have to deal with the most are disillusionment, which comes from sudden deflation, and bitterness, the result of prolonged blame. As you fly closer to the flame, the Spirit will help you come to terms with both.

Relational Concern

Now back to our story on Malta. The writer includes a couple of vignettes from the island that speak with relevance to us today.

> Now in the neighborhood of that place were lands belonging to the leading man of the island, named Publius, who welcomed us and entertained us courteously three days. And it came about that the father of Publius was lying in bed afflicted with recurrent fever and dysentery; and Paul went in to see him and after he had prayed, he laid his hands on him and healed him. And after this had happened, the rest of the people on the island who had diseases were coming to him

and getting cured. And they also honored us with many marks of respect; and when we were setting sail, they supplied us with all we needed.

Acts 28:7–10

Take a moment to notice the repeated pronouns "us" and "we." The writer of the narrative is obviously including himself. Who is he? Luke. And what is his profession? Physician. My point is this: Here is a physician, an educated, well-trained medical doctor whose expertise is the diagnosis of disease—in this case, "recurrent fever and dysentery," which caused Publius's father to be bedridden. Dr. Luke could diagnose the ailment, but he was at a loss to bring about a cure. Paul, however, as an apostle, possessed the supernatural, God-given ability to do what Luke could not do.

Instant Healing

Initially, Dr. Luke stood back as God worked through His servant Paul who, after praying for the afflicted man, "laid his hands on him and healed him." The word originally used by the physician-writer is *iaomai,* a Greek term that refers, more often than not, to instantaneous healing. Paul, please understand, was not the source of such power, only the vehicle . . . the human instrument through whom God supernaturally worked.

I am as impressed with Dr. Luke's lack of envy as I am with the apostle Paul's spiritual gift. The physician stepped aside. Although we may be certain his medical training left no room for divine miracles, his theology did! Without a moment's hesitation the professional was willing to stand back and watch God do the unusual.

And that last word is worth repeating for emphasis—an on-the-spot miracle is *unusual,* an exception to the general rule. As we have stated in the two previous chapters, there are times when God does indeed heal . . . instantly, miraculously, unexplainably. But, I repeat, such miracles are rare—unusual exceptions to the rule.

For too long people have been led to believe that in virtually every case they can "expect a miracle." And to make matters worse, when the miracle doesn't occur, they are told that something is wrong with them: they are harboring sin . . . they are not strong enough in their faith . . . and on and on. I shall restrain myself from grinding an ax at this point, but I must state that there are few areas in which there is greater confusion than this concept of instant healing. Sufferers are being promised miracles by many alleged authorities—some are sincere, some naive, some professional con artists—and when the miracle does not come, the damage done is always tragic and occasionally irreparable.

Prolonged Recovery

Look again at the last part of this account:

> And after this had happened, the rest of the people on the island who had diseases were coming to him and getting cured. And they also honored us with many marks of respect; and when we were setting sail, they supplied us with all we needed.
>
> Acts 28:9–10

As the word of that miracle traveled across the island, others with ailments came for healing. A cursory reading of what occurred could leave us with the impression that everyone who came received a similar instantaneous miracle. Not so. The original term used by Dr. Luke to describe the people's being "cured" is altogether different from the one he used for Publius's father. This word is *therapeuo,* from which we get our English word, "therapy." One reputable commentator writes that:

> *Healed* . . . might better be translated . . . *were treated.* It suggests not miraculous healings but medical treatment,

probably at the hands of Luke the physician. Verses 10 and 11 suggest that this medical ministry lasted through the three months stay at Malta.[3]

In other words, these people went through a process, a prolonged period of recovery, which lasted for three months—maybe longer.

Sometimes healing is instantaneous—*iaomai* recovery. More often than not, though, healing takes time—*therapeuo* recovery, under the care and watchful eyes of a competent physician. It is important to remember that the Holy Spirit is involved in both kinds of healings, not just the miraculous ones. Remember that! It is easy to overlook during the long and often anguishing months (sometimes years) of recovery.

Practical Lessons

We seldom think in terms of the lessons to be learned from, or the benefits connected to, prolonged recovery. As I mentioned earlier, we like quick turnarounds, instant changes from sickness to health. We much prefer hearing accounts of miracles as opposed to long, nonsensational stories of slow recoveries. In fact, we tend to be impatient with those who can't seem to take our advice and "snap out of it" or "get well soon," like the greeting card urges them to do. But like it or not, the wise words of Hippocrates are true: "Healing is a matter of time."

Respect . . . Rather Than Resentment

The one who needs time to heal, the individual who requires several months—perhaps, several years—to recover, is often the recipient of resentment. This works against the healing process. Instead of being affirmed and encouraged to press on through the pain, the sufferer encounters resentment, impatience, and uninvited advice that lacks understanding and reveals disrespect. The result is predictable.

This is especially true of those who must climb out of a background of emotional trauma. It took years for the damage to be done, yet many expect overnight recovery. For some there is the added stigma of attempted suicide or time spent in a psychiatric ward or mental hospital. For some their past has been strewn with the litter of a prison experience, a divorce, a rape, child abuse, molestation, or some other ego-shattering blow to their self-esteem. No one on the face of the earth would love to be healed quickly and get back in the mainstream of life more than these strugglers, but for them the therapy—the healing—is a prolonged and painful process, not an instant miracle.

Some, I realize, may go to extremes, play on our sympathy, and take advantage of our compassion. But more often than not, those who are recovering want nothing more than to be well, whole, responsible, functioning adults who carry their share of the load. Just as it is possible to hurry the very young through childhood, not giving them the benefit of growing up slowly and securely, so it is possible to hurry the very ill through recovery, robbing them of the benefits of healing slowly and permanently.

May I ask a favor? Please read that last sentence again, this time with feeling.

Wisdom . . . Not Just Knowledge

Now, let me speak directly to the sufferer for a moment. A major benefit of taking time to heal occurs within you where the Spirit is doing some of His best work. Almost imperceptibly, you are becoming a person with keener sensitivity, a broader base of understanding, and a longer fuse! Patience is a by-product of pain. So is tolerance with others and obedience before God. It is difficult to know how to classify these characteristics, but for lack of a better title, let's call the whole package *Spirit-given wisdom*.

For too many years in your life you may have operated strictly on the basis of knowledge . . . the human absorption of facts and natural reaction to others. But affliction has now entered your life, and even though you would much prefer to have it over with, it has not ended. The pain you are forced to endure is reshaping and remaking you deep within.

It is as David, the psalmist, once wrote:

> Before I was afflicted I went astray,
> But now I keep Thy word. . . .
> It is good for me that I was afflicted,
> That I may learn Thy statutes. . . .
> I know, O LORD, that Thy judgments are righteous,
> And that in faithfulness Thou hast afflicted me.
> Psalm 119:67, 71, 75

David admits that a much greater desire to obey (v. 67), a much more teachable spirit (v. 71), and a much less arrogant attitude (v. 75) were now his to claim, thanks to prolonged affliction.

Human knowledge comes naturally. It is enhanced by schooling and enlarged by travel. But with it there often comes carnal pride, a sense of self-sufficiency, and tough independence. This kind of knowledge can cause us to become increasingly less interested in the spiritual dimension of life. As our reservoir of horizontal knowledge grows, our skin gets thicker and often our inner being (called "the heart" in Scripture) becomes harder.

Then comes pain. Some physical ailment levels us to mere mortality. Or an emotional collapse. A domestic conflict explodes, and we are reduced to a cut above zero. The affliction (whatever it may be) paralyzes our productivity, and we are cast adrift in a sea of private turmoil and possibly public embarrassment. And to make matters worse, we are convinced we will never, ever recover.

At just such a dead-end street, divine wisdom waits to be embraced, bringing with it a beautiful blend of insight—the kind we never had with all our knowledge—genuine humility, a perception of others, and an incredible sensitivity toward God. During the time it is taking us to heal, wisdom is replacing knowledge. The vertical dimension is coming into clearer focus.

Balance . . . Freedom from Extremes

Finally, we cannot ignore the value of balance. I have already mentioned this concept several times in regard to other matters of the Spirit, but it plays an equally important role when it comes to healing. It has been my own experience, as well as my observation of others, that a lengthy recovery time rivets into our heads the importance of bringing our lives back from the fringes of the extreme. And I especially have in mind either the extreme of too much work (where our world is too structured, too product-oriented, too intense and responsible—to the point of neurosis) or too little work (where irresponsibility, inactivity, and indifference mark our paths). During the recovery stage, it is amazing how God enables us to see the foolish extremes of our former lives.

Eugene Peterson, in a work entitled *A Long Obedience in the Same Direction,* expresses well what I am trying to describe as he compares Western and Eastern cultures:

> The Christian has to find a better way to avoid the sin of Babel than by imitating the lilies of the field, who "neither toil nor spin." The pretentious work which became Babel and its pious opposite which developed at Thessalonica are displayed today on the broad canvasses of Western and Eastern cultures respectively.
>
> Western culture takes up where Babel left off and deifies human effort as such. The machine is the symbol of this way of life that attempts to control and manage. Technology promises to give us control over the earth and over other people. But the promise is not fulfilled: lethal automobiles, ugly buildings, and ponderous bureaucracies ravage the earth and empty lives of meaning. Structures become more important than the people who live in them. Machines become more important than the people who use them. We care more for our possessions with which we hope to make our way in the world than for our thoughts and dreams which tell us who we are in the world.

Eastern culture, on the other hand, is a variation on the Thessalonican view. There is a deep-rooted pessimism regarding human effort. Since all work is tainted with selfishness and pride, the solution is to withdraw from all activity into pure being. The symbol of such an attitude is the Buddha—an enormous fat person sitting cross-legged, looking at his own navel. Motionless, inert, quiet. All trouble comes from doing too much; therefore, do nothing. Step out of the rat race. The world of motion is evil, so quit doing everything. Say as little as possible; do as little as possible; finally, at the point of perfection, you will say nothing and do nothing. The goal is to withdraw absolutely and finally from action, from thought, from passion.

The two cultures are in collision today and many think that we must choose between them.[4]

As a result of this tendency toward extremes, many people break, and the inner destruction leaves them in shambles. It takes time to reorder and balance out our personal lives. Little wonder, then, that the Spirit does not always choose to work in a hurry.

There are many who teach that there is "healing in the atonement." By this they mean that the one who believes in Jesus Christ's atoning death for sin not only receives deliverance from sin but also deliverance from sin's by-products—sickness and disease. They base this teaching on Isaiah 53:5, a verse of Scripture that appears in a passage predicting the Messiah's death. Allow me to state the verse in its surrounding context.

> Surely our griefs He Himself bore,
> And our sorrows He carried;
> Yet we ourselves esteemed Him stricken,
> Smitten of God, and afflicted.
> But He was pierced through for our transgressions,
> He was crushed for our iniquities;
> The chastening for our well-being fell upon Him,
> And by His scourging we are healed.

All of us like sheep have gone astray,
Each of us has turned to his own way;
But the LORD has caused the iniquity of us all
To fall on Him.

He was oppressed and He was afflicted,
Yet He did not open His mouth;
Like a lamb that is led to slaughter,
And like a sheep that is silent before its shearers,
So He did not open His mouth.

                                Isaiah 53:4–7

A close and careful look at the prophet's words will reveal that the context is one of great physical pain that the Messiah would endure on the cross. But the point is this—His suffering is for our spiritual benefit. The subject being dealt with is the sinner's "transgressions," our "iniquities." The death of the Messiah provides the solution to our spiritual deadness. Our sins are forgiven because He once for all cleansed us when He was crucified. Hence, by His physical death, we are granted spiritual healing.

I agree that there is healing in the atonement . . . spiritual healing from the sins that kept us from God, healing from the overcoming power and influence of our adversary, healing from the grave that once frightened us, and healing from death that would otherwise conquer us.

And, of course, God promises to heal all of us of all illness and affliction once we pass from this life into glory. Such instant healing is part of the eternal package we receive when these bodies "put on immortality" (1 Cor. 15:53).

Our Response

There are several possible responses you may have to what I have written on the subjects of miracles, healings, and recovery.

First, it is possible that you honestly disagree with what I have presented. You are convinced that God works in a different way than I have described and that miracles are the rule, not the exception. I appreciate your open-minded attention, and I respect your right to disagree. My prayer is that God will comfort and encourage you as you trust Him to intervene. If He does, I will rejoice with you. If He does not, I hope you will not become disillusioned, confused, and bitter, as have so many I have dealt with who approached their situation from that perspective.

Second, you may find yourself encouraged and relieved because these things make sense. You agree that miracles can occur, healings do happen, but, more often than not, recovery takes time. And you are affirmed in the recovery process. Perhaps you were getting anxious and jumping to some false conclusions, misreading God's silence. You have decided to rest rather than strive. I am sincerely grateful that you have decided to "hang tough." Your renewed determination to learn and to grow through these stretching days will be *abundantly* rewarded. The roots grow deep when the winds are strong. Working through is always—always— more painful than walking out. But in the end, ah, what confident honesty, what calm assurance, what character depth!

Third, you may still be making up your mind. Some of this sounds reasonable. You identify and agree with several of the issues I have raised, but in the final analysis you are not ready to come down with both feet and say, "Yes, that's where I stand." You may be pleased (and surprised) to know that I consider this an intelligent response. The subject of pain is a profound one. The process involved in working through some of these issues is difficult, sometimes terribly complex. I may be able to address them in these few pages, but, believe me, in no way have I mastered the message I proclaim. How all these things fit together into God's perfect plans, I am not anywhere near prepared to say. Why human evil and its consequences are allowed such green lights by a holy God is another baffling paradox.

So my counsel to all, no matter how you respond to these last three chapters, is that you join me in continuing to search for answers. Let's listen to the wisdom of the Scriptures. Let's pay close attention to the "still small voice" of God who whispers to us in our pleasure and shouts to us in our pain. And most of all, let's not allow a few technical definitions or theological differences to push us apart. We still need each other.

It is difficult enough to handle life when we stand together. But doing battle with one another in addition to struggling through our shipwrecks, our Maltas, our storms, and our thorns can be almost unbearable. We need all the support we can get during recovery. As we take time to heal, let's also take time to hear . . . to care . . . to accept . . . to affirm one another.

12

Power, Power . . . We've Got the Power!

$\mathcal{A}$NY BOOK ON THE HOLY SPIRIT must give some space to the subject of power, since our Lord promised His disciples this one thing when the Spirit came upon them. Remember His words?

> "But you shall receive power when the Holy Spirit has come upon you; and you shall be My witnesses both in Jerusalem, and in all Judea and Samaria, and even to the remotest part of the earth."
>
> Acts 1:8

To those men, in that era, that heaven-sent, undeniable power from the One whom Jesus dispatched following His ascension manifested itself in dozens of different ways, many of them visible and supernatural. They were empowered to stand and preach before the public, unashamed and unafraid. They experienced such dynamic internal changes that they had the ability to speak in languages and dialects unknown to them. Some of them performed miraculous feats, others healed diseases instantly and permanently, discerned error, confronted evil, raised the dead, and endured the most torturous of deaths without flinching.

Something transformed those timid, awkward, fearful disciples into bold, devoted, inspiring men of God . . . and that something was *power*.

To be sure, that transitional interlude as the infant church was born and began to grow was a unique time. A time when miracles authenticated God's presence in human lives and God's message through human lips. Without the completed Scriptures, how would people know who were the anointed of God? Furthermore, in spreading the gospel rapidly across vast unevangelized regions, the ability to speak in many tongues was invaluable. Clearly, it took enormous power to launch the good ship *Ecclesia*.

But what about the power of the Spirit today? Can we—should we—expect "a miracle a day"? Should "supernatural power" be the watchword of every believer, whereby every one of us can expect "signs and wonders" on a regular basis? Is something wrong with us if we don't consistently witness or experience the Spirit of God's phenomenal presence and mighty workings? What are the evidences of Spirit-filled power today?

Let me set the record straight right away. In spite of what is being communicated these days, God's Word does not toss around the word *power* loosely; nor are we personally promised supernatural manifestations on a day-to-day basis. (As a friend of mine once said, "If miracles occurred every day, they wouldn't be called 'miracles' . . . they'd be called 'regulars.'") I have examined the Scriptures carefully and thoroughly for years, and nowhere do I find phenomenal demonstrations occurring on a daily basis in the lives of believers in biblical times. Neither then nor now could people expect to "name it and claim it." It is not only frustrating to people, it is erroneous to hold out such unrealistic expectations of incredible "power."

Today, however, power is in. There is "power evangelism" . . . "power prayer" . . . "power preaching" . . . "power healing" . . . "power encounters" and "power ministry" of every shape and size . . . even "power ties" available in various colors that "power ministers" can wear on "power Sundays." Talk about an overused, abused word! And the not-so-subtle message all this leaves is obvious: "If I'm not operating within the 'power' realm, something is missing from my life. I need to plug into this incredible 'power' source, so I, too, can tell amazing stories of mind-boggling miracles."

While I am just as interested in being a Spirit-filled minister of the gospel as anyone in God's family, I would caution all of the Lord's people against such unrealistic and unbiblical expectations. Power is promised us, yes, and in the person of the Holy Spirit we do have the source of that power within us—all of us do! But in no way does this mean that with the snap of our fingers we can expect to invoke some supernatural manifestation. It doesn't work like that . . . it never did!

Understanding First Things First

Let's return to basics . . . two foundational issues we touched on earlier. One has to do with salvation, the other with being Spirit-filled.

How would you complete these two sentences?

- I am a Christian because _____.
- I am filled with the Spirit when _____.

What does it mean to be a Christian? How can a person say with assurance that he or she is a member of God's forever family? Let's allow God's Word to answer that for us.

> But as many as received Him, to them He gave the right to become children of God, even to those who believe in His name.
>
> John 1:12

A little later, John's Gospel records Jesus' conversation with a man who had questions about how he could have eternal life with God.

> Jesus answered and said to him, "Truly, truly, I say to you, unless one is born again, he cannot see the kingdom of God. . . . That which is born of the flesh is flesh, and that which is born of the Spirit is spirit. Do not marvel that I said

to you, 'You must be born again.' The wind blows where it wishes and you hear the sound of it, but do not know where it comes from and where it is going; so is everyone who is born of the Spirit."

John 3:3, 6–8

"He who believes in the Son has eternal life; but he who does not obey the Son shall not see life, but the wrath of God abides on him."

John 3:36

Is it that narrow? Is becoming a Christian limited solely to knowing Christ? Again, let's let Jesus answer that for us.

Jesus said to him, "I am the way, and the truth, and the life; no one comes to the Father, but through Me."

John 14:6

That is an exclusive statement, no question about it. But the truth is as narrow as Christ has declared it, and it is truth because He said it. The first sentence I asked you to complete could read as follows: I am a Christian because *I am rightly related to the Son of God*. Later in the New Testament we read similar words as those we just looked at in the Gospel by John.

For there is one God, and one mediator also between God and men, the man Christ Jesus.

1 Timothy 2:5

And the witness is this, that God has given us eternal life, and this life is in His Son. He who has the Son has the life; he who does not have the Son of God does not have the life.

1 John 5:11–12

Very simple. Very clear. People are not born right with God. That is why everyone who hopes to spend eternity with Him must be born from above, born anew spiritually. Furthermore, people do not become Christians because they go to church or because they have been christened as babies or because they have been dedicated as children or because they have been baptized or because they are sincere and mean well and pay their bills. Becoming a Christian has nothing to do with what we do or with how hard we work. No, it's a matter of grace, not works.

> For by grace you have been saved through faith; and that not of yourselves, it is the gift of God; not as a result of works, that no one should boast.
>
> Ephesians 2:8–9

Let me illustrate. I have a book in my hand. If I were to hand it to you and say, "It's yours; I'd like you to have it," and you were to take it, I would be giving you a gift. When you take the gift, you become the possessor of what was once mine. Because you took it, it's yours.

Likewise, salvation is a gift. God reached out to you and me at the cross, where His Son paid the penalty of sin by dying in our place, and He gave us eternal life in His Son. All He asks is that we reach out in faith and take His gift.

And so . . . how does one become a Christian? By being rightly related to Jesus Christ, the Son of God. This is Salvation 101. It's as basic as you can get.

What must I do then to get the source of God's power into my life? This may surprise you, but the answer is *nothing*. He comes to live within you when you believe in Christ. You don't make a single contribution to your standing before God by doing this or promising that or giving up certain things. The transaction is based on grace—God's matchless, unmerited favor. When you and I receive the gift of eternal life, wrapped inside that gift is the Holy Spirit. He comes as part of the "initial salvation package." We are never commanded to pray for the Holy Spirit or to be baptized by the Holy Spirit or to be regenerated by the Holy Spirit or to be sealed by the Holy Spirit. Why? Because all of those things occur at the moment we are born anew.

So you have in your hands the book I gave you as a gift. Now, what if you were to say to me, "I would really, really love to have every chapter of this book." I would answer, "You have all the chapters. They are all there and they are all yours to read and enjoy. You have the book; therefore you have everything in it." So it is with Christ. Upon receiving Him, we have everything that comes with the gift of salvation . . . and that certainly includes the person of the Holy Spirit.

> For even as the body is one and yet has many members, and all the members of the body, though they are many, are one body, so also is Christ. For by one Spirit we were all baptized into one body, whether Jews or Greeks, whether slaves or free, and we were all made to drink of one Spirit.
>
> 1 Corinthians 12:12–13

And because we have the Spirit, the source of power is within us.

This brings me to the second sentence I asked you to complete, which could read: I am filled with the Spirit when *I am rightly related to the Spirit of God.*

When we are, the "power" within us is unleashed and we become His vessels of honor, ready and available for whatever service He wishes us to perform. When filled, the "power" that raised Christ from the dead becomes the motivating force behind our lives. Think of it! It was this very power Paul referred to when he wrote of his deep desire to fly closer to the flame:

> [For my determined purpose is] that I may know Him—that I may progressively become more deeply and intimately acquainted with Him, perceiving and recognizing and understanding [the wonders of His Person] more strongly and more clearly. And that I may in that same way come to know the power outflowing from His resurrection [which it exerts over believers]; and that I may so share His sufferings as to be continually transformed [in spirit into His likeness even] to His death.
>
> Philippians 3:10 AMP

The filling of the Spirit not only means that our lives are totally available to God, but it also includes such things as keeping short accounts, being sensitive to whatever may have come between us and Him . . . and walking in complete dependence upon Him.

When we do, He is able to work through us, speak through us, use us, direct us without restraint, and empower our gifts and our efforts in ways we could never accomplish on our own. It isn't that we need more of the Spirit (an impossibility); it is that we need His power, His working, His cleansing, His freeing. And as He fills us, all that and so much more take place.

To return to the P word: The Christian life is not some kind of ecstatic "power life" with hour-by-hour, day-after-day phenomenal experiences. The blessed Spirit of God does not provide "power surges" of incredible proportions.

Am I saying He never causes phenomenal, even miraculous things to occur? No. But what I am saying is that when He does, it is the exception rather than the rule. Our Lord is not in competition with Fantasyland.

My concern is that we have as realistic and relevant a view of this as the Scriptures allow—and nothing more. But make no mistake about it, when it comes to power, power . . . we've got the power!

Understanding the Continual, Normal
Evidences of the Spirit's Empowering

So, then, you may ask, "What is this realistic and relevant view of the Christian life? What can I expect to see as continual and normal evidences of Christ in my life?" Numerous things come to mind.

Because I am a Christian and therefore rightly related to the Son of God:

- I am in Christ.
- I live in Him and He lives in me.

- I know the relief of being cleansed from personal sins.
- I am able to live above sin's dominating control.
- I have immediate access to the Father through prayer.
- I can understand the Scriptures.
- I am able to forgive—and should forgive—whoever wrongs me.
- I have the capacity to bear fruit, daily, continually, routinely.
- I possess at least one (sometimes more than one) spiritual gift.
- I worship with joy and with purpose.
- I find the church vital, not routine or boring.
- I have a faith to share with others.
- I love and need other people.
- I look forward to having close fellowship with fellow Christians.
- I am able to obey the teaching of the Word of God.
- I continue to learn and grow toward maturity.
- I can endure suffering and hardship without losing heart.
- I depend and trust in my Lord for daily strength and provisions.
- I can know God's will.
- I live in anticipation of Christ's return.
- I have the assurance of heaven after I die.

This list could continue for pages, but perhaps this sampling will alert you to the fact that these are the kinds of unique possessions, experiences, and blessings that are ours by God's grace to enjoy simply because we have been accepted into His family. They are ours to claim every day. And when we add them all together, they represent an impressive list of incredible realities.

While none of the above would be considered miraculous—at least in the usual sense of the term—they are certainly remarkable. And when we remind ourselves that these are normal and continually ours to enjoy, the Christian life becomes the most enviable lifestyle one can imagine.

This may not be "power Christianity," but it is certainly the "abundant life" Christ promised. Get that straight . . . or you will live your life disappointed and frustrated, always looking for something more ecstatic or supernatural in nature.

Several years ago a pilot told me that flying an airplane consists of hours and hours of sheer boredom, interrupted periodically with split seconds of sheer panic.

I would never use the word *boredom* to describe the Christian life, but you get the point. God can (and sometimes does) step into our world in supernatural ways and manifest His power. It is remarkable how on occasion He interrupts the routine (if we could call the things I listed routine) with something phenomenal that only He could have done. We acknowledge that and praise Him for it . . . but, I repeat, we should not expect that day after day.

In some ways, the normal Christian life is not unlike the normal married life. The normal married life is not soft music, Saran-Wrap negligees, and night-after-night in a bubbly hot tub. The normal married life is not soft-footed waiters serving you tea in the afternoon at the Ritz-Carlton Hotel while you watch the surf break on Maui. It's not letters in the mail several times a month announcing that you and your mate have won $50 million in the lottery jackpot. It's not a husband coming home with flowers every afternoon. It's not $500 gift certificates to Nordstroms each Saturday morning. It's not happy, carefree teenagers anxious to help with the dishes and thrilled to keep their rooms clean. It's not a mother-in-law with a face like Michelle Pfeiffer and a heart like Mother Teresa.

If you are a bride- or groom-to-be anticipating that, I've got only three words for you. *Get a life!* Visit with any married couple for a day or two (especially those with small children), and you will come back to reality real fast.

In the same way, some Fantasyland concept of Christianity frustrates much more than it thrills. The wide-eyed, smiling televangelist won't tell you this, but I'm giving you the straight scoop.

So much for a quick summary of the Christian life. Now how about the Spirit-filled life? Let me suggest another list for you to ponder. These are things you and I can claim when the Spirit is in full control.

When we are Spirit-filled and therefore rightly related to the Spirit of God:

- We are surrounded by the Spirit's omnipotent shield of protection, continually and routinely.

- We have an inner dynamic to handle life's pressures.

- We are able to be joyful . . . regardless.

- We have the capacity to grasp the deep things of God that He discloses to us in His Book.

- We have little difficulty maintaining a positive attitude of unselfishness, servanthood, and humility.

- We have a keen sense of intuition and discernment; we sense evil.

- We are able to love and be loved in return.

- We can be vulnerable and open.

- We can rely on the Spirit to intercede for us when we don't even know how to pray as we should.

- We need never fear evil or demonic and satanic assault.

- We are enabled to stand alone with confidence.

- We experience inner assurance regarding decisions as well as right and wrong.

- We have an "internal filtering system."

- We can actually live worry-free.

- We are able to minister to others through our spiritual gift(s).

- We have an intimate, abiding "Abba relationship" with the living God.

When I buried my dad, who outlived my mother by nine years, for the first time I found myself feeling alone, even though I was an adult and a father of four. While feeling strangely and suddenly "orphaned," the thought dawned on me that I have the Spirit of God to be my constant companion and counselor for the rest of my life. How wonderful! He lives as a permanent resident. His earthly address is my body!

Again, none of the things on the list above could be called phenomenal . . . they are neither miraculous in nature nor supernatural manifestations . . . but they are ours to claim simply because the powerful Spirit of God is filling us. This is not "power filling," but the normal, albeit wonderful, Spirit-filled life.

And frankly, these evidences are the kinds of things we need and can count on far more than those exceptional moments of sheer ecstasy. These are the things we can count on because we are rightly related to the Son of God and to the Spirit of God. We do not need continual, highly charged "power visions" or "power encounters" nearly as much as we need to be filled with the sustaining, all-powerful Spirit of God.

I say again, power, power . . . we've got the power! Who does? Every child of God who walks in the power of the Holy Spirit. When we do, we are "freed up" to enjoy incredible release from the things that would otherwise hold us in bondage. What great liberty!

> Now the Lord is the Spirit; and where the Spirit of the Lord is, there is liberty.
>
> 2 Corinthians 3:17

Just look at that promise.

Liberty is another word for freedom. Freedom from what? Freedom from constraint and from fear. Freedom from tedious perfectionism. Freedom from a confining, boring, predictable life. Freedom from bondage. Freedom from addictions. Freedom to be, to do, to become. And such freedom comes from simply having the Spirit and allowing Him to fill us. Again, it is not "power freedom." It is a quiet, gentle release from all that binds us so that we can be whole, completely authentic. When in grief, we are free to cry. When experiencing joy, we are free to laugh.

Admitting Occasional Exceptional Experiences

Am I saying that we never experience the miraculous? I am not. Or that we should consider all supernatural manifestations today as coming from the devil? No. I am suggesting, however, that we be discerning. He is God. He can do anything, anytime, anywhere. That is His prerogative.

Many times people come to me and say, "Would you pray for so-and-so?" and they will name a wife, a husband, a mother, a dad, a child, or a friend who's dying. Doctors have given up hope and encouraged them not to expect anything but death. So they ask, "Would you just pray for that person?" My answer invariably is, "Yes, of course." And I do. But beyond that I really have no right to promise those people that their loved ones will be healed and live. Not being God and not knowing God's specific will, I pray for God's glory to be manifested. I pray that if it is His will He might bring about a miraculous healing. And I pray that He will give strength to those who wait and minister to the dying. But I have no right to make a "power promise." *Neither does anyone else!*

Let me remind you that when we talk about the Spirit of God, we are not talking about a small part of the whole. The Spirit of God is, in fact, God. And as a member of the Godhead, He is incomprehensible and infinite in nature. His work can seem mysterious, and at times His presence, terribly obscure. Humanly speaking, I sometimes feel His plan is a bit confusing and illogical. (But that's my problem, not His.) Because I cannot unravel His divine tapestry or explain in detail the work of His hands, it does not mean that there is something wrong with His plan.

Zophar the Naamathite said to Job in utter despair, "Can we by searching find out God?" The implication is no.

And since this is true, let's let God be God. Let's not feel that we must explain every part of Him or defend His plan or describe His will to the nth degree. We would do well to employ three words on a regular basis: "I don't know."

With these things in mind, I conclude this chapter with three final thoughts:

First, *God is the God of the miraculous.* Please do not misquote or misrepresent me by saying that Swindoll does not believe in the miraculous. God is God; therefore, miracles fall from His hands. They do occur. But let's be true to the Scriptures and correctly state that those miracles are the exceptions, not the norm. They aren't "regulars." Nor do they occur on command. They occur when God, in His marvelous, mysterious, inscrutable plan, causes them to happen.

Second, *God is the God of the supernatural.* Again, Scripture suggests that supernatural phenomena are occasional, not routine. But be careful what you tag "miraculous" or "phenomenal." Don't toss those words around loosely. It's like the word "awesome." Everything today is awesome. Ballplayers are awesome! Toyotas are awesome! Nonsense. Only God is awesome. And if He is pleased to carry out some phenomenal manifestation, I stand back and applaud it and would not even attempt to explain it . . . and certainly not act as though I caused it.

Third, *God is the God of the mysterious.* Because He is God, He can—and does—cause things to occur that we cannot explain. However, I remind you again, such mysteries are occasional and exceptional. To quote A. W. Tozer:

> Left to ourselves we tend immediately to reduce God to manageable terms. We want to get Him where we can use Him, or at least know where He is when we need Him. We want a God we can in some measure control. We need the feeling of security that comes from knowing what God is like, and what He is like is of course a composite of all the

religious pictures we have seen, all the best people we have known or heard about, and all the sublime ideas we have entertained.

If all this sounds strange to modern ears, it is only because we have for a full half century taken God for granted. The glory of God has not been revealed to this generation of men. The God of contemporary Christianity is only slightly superior to the gods of Greece and Rome, if indeed He is not actually inferior to them, in that He is weak and helpless while they at least had power.

If what we conceive God to be He is not, how then shall we think of Him? If He is indeed incomprehensible, as the Creed declares Him to be, and unapproachable, as Paul says He is, how can we Christians satisfy our longing after Him? The hopeful words, "Acquaint now thyself with him, and be at peace," still stand after the passing of the centuries; but how shall we acquaint ourselves with One who eludes all the straining efforts of mind and heart? And how shall we be held accountable to know what cannot be known? . . .

The answer of the Bible is simply "through Jesus Christ our Lord." In Christ and by Christ, God effects complete self-disclosure, although He shows Himself not to reason but to faith and love. Faith is an organ of knowledge, and love an organ of experience. God came to us in the incarnation; in atonement He reconciled us to Himself, and by faith and love we enter and lay hold on Him.

"Verily God is of infinite greatness," says Christ's enraptured troubadour, Richard Rolle; "more than we can think; . . . unknowable by created things; and can never be comprehended by us as He is in Himself. But even here and now, whenever the heart begins to burn with a desire for God, she is made able to receive the uncreated light and, inspired and fulfilled by the gifts of the Holy Ghost, she tastes the joys of heaven.[1]

I have a very good friend whose son has been through an incredibly difficult period of illness. I have ached with him and his wife, and Cynthia and I have prayed for them frequently in the last few months. For a while nothing was going right. Things that were bad only got worse. They faced a wall of impossibilities they could not scale. And then—a breakthrough occurred. They were put in touch with a specialist, a gifted, insightful physician who, through a particular technique, introduced them to the source of the problem. And this little fellow who had been laid aside for months is now well on his way to full recovery, for which we praise our sovereign God and His empowering Spirit.

It would be the tendency of some to cry, "Miraculous!" No, it was no miracle. It was, in fact, a delicate, scientific, carefully honed procedure of diagnosis and treatment that worked on the boy. Was God in it? Absolutely. Doctors diagnose and treat; God alone can heal. God, in powerful grace, led in the finding of the physician. God prompted another person to provide all the finances since the couple had meager resources. And God used the procedure to heal the boy's life.

His power was evident from start to finish . . . but it was no "power healing." What happened? Several of us joined our hearts with our friends and decided to fly closer to the flame as together we trusted Him who has all the power to do whatever is best. It happened quietly, slowly, thoroughly . . . and powerfully.

13

Is That All There Is to the Spirit's Ministry?

*I*N MY ALMOST SIXTY YEARS on this old earth, I have discovered that one of the best ways to arrive at the right answers is to start with the right questions. And so I have come to this vast subject of the Holy Spirit with more searching questions than hard-and-fast answers. Maybe that is what first attracted me to a disarming little book titled *Dear God: Children's Letters to God*.

A little girl named Lucy asks God: "Dear God, are You really invisible or is that just a trick?"

Norma asks: "Dear God, did You mean for a giraffe to look like that or was that an accident?"

One of my favorites was asked by Nan: "Dear God, who draws the lines around all the countries?"

And Neil writes: "Dear God, I went to this wedding and they kissed right in church. Is that okay?"

Lois asks, "Dear God, I like the Lord's prayer best of all. Did You have to write it a lot or did You get it right the first time?"

From Joanne, "I would like to know why all the things You said are in red."

Darla asks, "Did You really mean *Do unto others as they do unto you*? Because if You did, then I'm going to fix my brother."

Peter requests, "Will You please send Dennis Clark to a different camp this year?"

And Anita asks, "Is it true my father won't get in heaven if he uses his bowling words in the house?"[1]

Hilarious, charming, innocent . . . and oh, so perceptive! Don't you wrestle at times with questions that flip through your mind and snag in one of those creases up there? I certainly do! And let's be painfully candid and honest about it, most of us have many more questions than we do absolute answers . . . just like these children.

Most folks don't make me nervous, but those who do are the ones who have convinced themselves that they have pretty well buttoned up all the theological hatches. They see themselves as answer-givers rather than question-askers. You have a problem? Just ask; they'll unload the truck on you. And especially important to them is that you be impressed with their storehouse of knowledge. What bothers me most, though, is their lack of childlike curiosity . . . for "children" of God, that's pretty arrogant. Most of the answer-givers have stopped asking the hard questions. Their arrogance has not only stopped their ears, it has closed their minds.

That's not the case with Seymour. I've saved his question for last: "Dear God, How come You did all those miracles in the old days and You don't do any now?"[2]

Anyone who studies the lives of Moses or Elijah or Jesus is haunted by that question. Recorded in the pages of the Great Book are back-to-back phenomenal events and miraculous moments during the lifetimes of those three. But how rarely they occur today. "Dear God, have those things ended? Is that all there is to the Spirit's ministry? If things have changed so, have we reached the end of His powerful presence and workings?"

Evidences of His Presence

Remember early on in the book when we looked at Jesus' words to His faithful few just before He was grabbed by a mob, rushed through a series of trials, and hammered to a cross? We heard Him promise that even though He was leaving, He would not leave them as orphans.

> "And I will ask the Father, and He will give you another Helper, that He may be with you forever."
> John 14:16

He had been their Helper all along their three-plus years to-gether. When they needed anything, all they had to do was say, "Jesus," and He would be there to help. "Lord, we weren't able to cast out demons." So He said, "Stand back. Let me show how this is done." Or "Lord, we reached this impasse and we weren't able to—" "Let Me help you with that." He had been their Helper . . . but no longer.

Now He promises "Another Helper," for which John uses the term that meant "Another of the same kind." And so when we ask, "Is that all there is?" the answer is no, we haven't reached the end of the Spirit's era. Jesus promised His disciples directly . . . and us indirectly: "He will be there forever." And who is this next Helper?

> "That is the Spirit of truth, whom the world cannot receive, because it does not behold Him or know Him, but you know Him because He abides with you, and will be in you."
> John 14:17

Jesus was suggesting a new, much more intimate relation-ship. In effect, He was saying, "You've been engaged to Him during My earthly ministry, but when I leave you're going to be married to Him. So far it's been like dating. When I leave and He comes, it will be like marriage. It won't be a distant, formal rela-tionship where the two of you go home separately every night to different places. No, there will be a permanent intimacy, a one-ness. In fact, He will live in you forever."

A few minutes later He assured them:

> "But I tell you the truth, it is to your advantage that I go away; for if I do not go away, the Helper shall not come to you; but if I go, I will send Him to you."
> John 16:7

And then He added:

> "But when He, the Spirit of truth, comes, He will guide you into all the truth; for He will not speak on His own initiative,

but whatever He hears, He will speak; and He will disclose to you what is to come."

John 16:13

They would need help to get through the tough spots, and He, the Spirit, would be there to provide that assistance.

When I was in the marines, in January 1958 our troopship sailed into Yokohama harbor. Though years had passed since the end of World War II, that harbor was still a place of danger because of underwater mines that had not yet been removed. At the mouth of the harbor, our ship stopped and took aboard a Japanese harbor pilot to lead us through the treacherous waters. Slowly and cautiously he steered us through those dark, uncharted waters. As we stood on deck, we could see nothing but the surface below us and the harbor ahead of us. But the harbor pilot steered the ship with confidence, knowing every turn to take to bring us safely to the pier.

In the same way, our Lord promised that the Helper would guide us into all the truth, steering us through life, pointing out the shoals and the reefs and the mines ahead. While we see only the surface, He sees into the depths and beyond the horizon.

As we have discovered in earlier chapters, the Spirit of God works deeply and intimately to transform our lives. He passionately desires to direct our steps, cleanse our thoughts, heal our wounds, take over our worries, reveal God's will, and protect us from evil. All this and so much more is ours through the dynamic presence of the One whom Jesus sent to be our Helper.

Have we reached the end . . . is that all there is to the Spirit's ministry? The answer is a resounding No! Absolutely not! Within us and around us every day we see evidences of His dynamic power.

We see the Spirit at work in our lives. We can know the Spirit's presence by witnessing it in our own lives. His work is continually going on. Paul states very clearly that our bodies represent the Spirit's temple:

> Or do you not know that your body is a temple of the Holy
> Spirit who is in you, whom you have from God, and that you
> are not your own? For you have been bought with a price:
> therefore glorify God in your body.
>
> 1 Corinthians 6:19–20

> The Spirit Himself bears witness with our spirit that we are
> children of God, and if children, heirs also, heirs of God and
> fellow heirs with Christ, if indeed we suffer with Him in or-
> der that we may also be glorified with Him.
>
> Romans 8:16–17

When we are with other Christians, the witness of the Spirit
verifies our spiritual connection, even though we may speak different languages and come from differing cultures. It's a wonderful connection. I can sit down with a body of believers in Russia
and feel an immediate sense of accord . . . a family identification
. . . and yet I don't speak a word of Russian. That is the Spirit's
work.

Furthermore, when we encounter enemy attacks, the Spirit's
work is evident because there is a sense of confidence and security
in our faith.

> You are from God, little children, and have overcome them;
> because greater is He who is in you than he who is in the
> world.
>
> 1 John 4:4

We see the Spirit empowering gifted Christians for ministry. Those
gifts and ministries differ and vary, but the same Holy Spirit is at
work.

> Now there are varieties of gifts, but the same Spirit. And
> there are varieties of ministries, and the same Lord. And there
> are varieties of effects, but the same God who works all things
> in all persons. But to each one is given the manifestation of
> the Spirit for the common good.
>
> 1 Corinthians 12:4–7

When I hear a gifted teacher expound the Scriptures, I am benefiting from the Spirit's work in that person's life. When I hear of or see people gifted in evangelism winning people to Christ, I know the work of the Spirit is involved. When I see people showing mercy and encouragement, demonstrating hospitality, and helping others, I am witnessing the work of the Spirit.

We see the Spirit restraining lawlessness.

> For the mystery of lawlessness is already at work; only he who now restrains will do so until he is taken out of the way. And then that lawless one will be revealed whom the Lord will slay with the breath of His mouth and bring to an end by the appearance of His coming.
>
> 2 Thessalonians 2:7–8

Now, I can hear your immediate reaction. "What? Restraining lawlessness? Have you looked at the headlines lately?" And granted, the world does seem chaotic and out of control. Lawlessness appears to be at an all-time high. But think about it . . . What would this world be like if the controlling influence of the Spirit of God were lifted from this earth? Think about what it would be like if all the believers, empowered with the Spirit of God, suddenly disappeared. When the restrainer (the controlling power of the Spirit) is removed, there will be expressions and outbreaks of evil like we have never witnessed.

We may think, *It can't get any worse.* But it will. When the restrainer is lifted from this earth, it will indeed! But for now we know His work is evident because He continues to restrain lawlessness.

Finally, *we see the Spirit regenerating the lost.* He is still expanding the ranks of the church. Remember Jesus' words?

> "Truly, truly, I say to you, unless one is born again, he cannot see the kingdom of God. . . . That which is born of the flesh is flesh, and that which is born of the Spirit is spirit. Do not marvel that I said to you, 'You must be born again.'"
>
> John 3:3, 6–8

The Spirit is still at work, leading people to Christ . . . still building His church.

Recently I got a letter I was tempted to frame! It is from a young physician. And as you read these excerpts, remember . . . you are reading about the work of the Spirit on one person's life. Imagine the thousands of stories that could be written every day!

Not too long ago I finished a rotation at the Loma Linda Veterans Hospital and one of my patients was in the Navy during World War II. He served in the Battle of Midway and was on the USS *Lexington* which was sunk in that battle. The individual I met was literally just a skeleton of the man who fought for our country. He now was on the losing end of a battle against a certain type of lung cancer that is well known as being the most deadly and the most rapidly fatal type of lung cancer. The malignancy is usually located near the mainstem bronchus which is the main "tube" that brings air into each lung, so as the tumor grows it will progressively suffocate the patient. In addition to slowly suffocating, the patient will also suffer indescribable bone pain secondary to the cancer's propensity to spread to bones throughout the body. . . .

[This disease] is brought on by hard living and excessive smoking, which was exactly the history of this patient. Because you too were once a "military man," you will know what I am describing when I say that this patient used to be as tough as nails, feared nothing, and lived life with incredible reckless abandon. However, forty years of hard living had caught up and had beaten him. He now weighed less than ninety pounds (in his prime he weighed close to two hundred pounds), he was unable to sit up in bed secondary to severe weakness and pain, he had lost all of his hair secondary to chemotherapy. He was only able to speak a few words at a time, otherwise he would get too short of breath.

I knew after my first talk with him that he would not live another week. I am not the type of medical student who usually shares Christianity to patients, but this man was an exception. After taking time to build a relationship with him, I asked him if he were afraid of dying. He stated that he had absolutely no fear of death. I was shocked by his confidence because at this point I only knew of his military days, and I figured that he was just giving me a "tough guy" image (but I should have known that people on their deathbed usually cease seeing the need to be false). But he continued and told me the events of his life, and because he had to take many pauses to catch his breath, this took quite a while.

He rehashed to me his wild Navy days during the war up until the point two years ago when he was in the depths of depression and feelings of hopelessness. He was living back east at the time, he had been divorced several times, and did not know where his children were living, and he was now living all alone. He was at the point of considering suicide when on the radio came a program he had never heard before. He stated that the show was entitled "Insight for Living." He said that right then and there, after listening to only this one show, he accepted Christ into his life as his personal Savior. He later moved out to Orange County, California, but he never did attend the First Evangelical Free Church of Fullerton because he was too embarrassed of his past life to go to the church that Chuck Swindoll spoke at. At this point I took the liberty of telling him that you too used to be in the military, and I told him that Chuck Swindoll would have been proud to meet him because he was a genuine Christian. . . . At this statement, he smiled the biggest smile possible.

Our conversation came to a close at this point and I told him that I would see him the next morning. However, during the night, he fell into a coma and died two days later, never regaining consciousness.[3]

The Spirit of God did all that! Just think . . . one voice from the middle of nowhere, one statement, and a man's whole life is regenerated.

Yes, the Spirit is still at work transforming lives. He is still touching people. Still using folks like you and me. The Spirit of

God is very much alive and well on Planet Earth. His ministry is far from over!

Few people could express my closing thoughts on the Holy Spirit better than the late, great Charles Haddon Spurgeon:

> Common, too common is the sin of forgetting the Holy Spirit. This is folly and ingratitude. . . . As God, He is good essentially. . . . He is good benevolently, tenderly bearing with our waywardness, striving with our rebellious wills; quickening us from our death in sin, and then training us for the skies as a loving nurse fosters her child. . . . He is good operatively. All His works are good in the most eminent degree: He suggests good thoughts, prompts good actions, reveals good truths, applies good promises, assists in good attainments, and leads to good results. There is no spiritual good in all the world of which He is not the author and sustainer. . . . They who yield to His influence become good; they who obey His impulses do good, they who live under His power receive good. . . . Let us revere His person, and adore Him as God over all, blessed for ever; let us own His power, and our need of Him by waiting upon Him in all our holy enterprises; let us hourly seek His aid, and never grieve Him; and let us speak to His praise whenever occasions occur. The church will never prosper until more reverently it believes in the Holy Ghost.[4]

May these chapters not only help you understand the work and enter into the power of the Holy Spirit, but, more than that, may they lead you to the most exciting and fulfilling experience in life . . . flying closer to the flame.

Epilogue

Throughout this book, I have encouraged you to stay open and teachable, and I appreciate your willingness to do so. But I have also warned you of the need to guard yourself against error, that you not be swept up into movements and groups and extremes that will hurt you and disillusion you rather than help, encourage, and strengthen you. So as we look forward to flying closer to the flame as the Spirit of God controls and transforms our lives, we need to keep a few practical and helpful checkpoints in mind.

Checkpoint 1: *Always let your Bible be your guide.* Whenever you are in doubt or confusion, always go back to the Bible. Anytime you are not sure . . . or feel uneasy . . . or wonder if something may not be quite right—it's the Bible you need to consult.

Checkpoint 2: *Be discerning.* It pays to be a little suspicious, even a tad skeptical. To keep asking questions. To check out the character of the one doing the teaching. Don't be gullible. Keep thinking clearly. Be discerning.

Checkpoint 3: *Stay balanced.* In other words, guard against extremism. If you find things getting a little fanatical, put on the brakes. Christ builds His body with stable, contagious Christians. Fanatics are not contagious, they are frightening. If you are alienating those who are strong in their walk with Christ, something is wrong. If you have been following someone's teaching and things are starting to get a little weird, pay attention to that "unidentified inner prompting."

One other little tip on staying balanced: If you are becoming more and more exclusive, you are probably moving toward error.

When God's in it, He blends the flow of truth into the whole body of Christ. If you are beginning to think you have a corner on what's right, something's wrong. You are losing your balance.

Checkpoint 4: *Seek the counsel of men and women you admire.* If you are beginning to wonder about what's being taught, spend some time with those who are not caught up in the things you have been hearing and following. You need a calm, objective, wise perspective. Seek it out.

Checkpoint 5: *Keep the unity.* Keeping the unity of the Spirit is not simply a nice option, it is a biblical command to keep the body strong. It is an essential part of our walk. Don't allow yourself to be deliberately divisive. There are a few occasions when one must stand alone and walk away, but those times are exceptions, not the rule.

Notes

Chapter 1
Let's Get Acquainted with the Spirit

1. Archibald Thomas Robertson, *The Acts of the Apostles,* vol. 3. of *Word Pictures in the New Testament* (Nashville, Tenn.: Broadman Press, 1930), 10.
2. F. F. Bruce, *Commentary on the Book of Acts* (Grand Rapids, Mich.: Eerdmans, 1954), 38–39.

Chapter 2
The Main Agenda of God's Spirit: Transformation

1. Robert E. Coleman, *The Master Plan of Evangelism* (Old Tappan, N.J.: Revell, 1964), 23.
2. Ibid., 22–23.
3. Max DePree, *Leadership Jazz* (New York: Doubleday, 1992), 14–15.

Chapter 3
My Sin . . . and "The Things of the Spirit"

1. J. B. Phillips, *Your God Is Too Small* (New York: Macmillan, 1987).
2. Martin Lloyd-Jones, as quoted in and reprinted from John White, *When the Spirit Comes with Power* (Downers Grove, Ill.: InterVarsity Press, 1988), 13. Used by permission of InterVarsity Press, P.O. Box 1400, Downers Grove, Ill. 60515.

Chapter 4
Is the Spirit's Filling That Big a Deal?

1. John R. W. Stott, *Baptism and Fullness: The Work of the Holy Spirit Today* (Downers Grove, Ill.: InterVarsity Press, n.d.), 57.

2. Ibid.

3. C. S. Lewis, *Christian Reflections,* ed. Walter Hooper (Grand Rapids, Mich.: Eerdmans, 1974), preface.

Chapter 6
Draw Me Nearer . . . Nearer

1. A personal letter. Used by permission.

2. Archibald Thomas Robertson, *The Acts of the Apostles,* vol. 3. of *Word Pictures in the New Testament* (Nashville, Tenn.: Broadman Press, 1930), 76.

3. Clark H. Pinnock, "Our Source of Authority: The Bible," *Bibliotheca Sacra,* vol. 124, no. 494 (April-June 1967): 150, 151.

4. Fanny J. Crosby, 1875.

Chapter 7
Those Unidentified Inner Promptings

1. A. Cohen, *The Psalms* (London: Soncino Press, 1958), 453.

2. C. F. Keil and F. Delitzsch, *The Books of the Kings,* in *Biblical Commentary on the Old Testament,* trans. James Martin (Grand Rapids, Mich.: Eerdmans, n.d.), 258.

3. "How Firm a Foundation," *Rippons Selection of Hymns,* 1787.

Chapter 8
The Spirit and Our Emotions

1. John White, *When the Spirit Comes with Power: Signs and Wonders Among God's People* (Downers Grove, Ill.: InterVarsity Press, 1988), 48, 49. Used by permission of InterVarsity Press, P.O. Box 1400, Downers Grove, Ill. 60515

Chapter 9
Thinking Theologically About Sickness and Healing

1. John White, *When the Spirit Comes with Power: Signs and Wonders Among God's People* (Downers Grove, Ill.: InterVarsity Press, 1988),

17–18. Used by permission of InterVarsity Press, P.O. Box 1400, Downers Grove, Ill. 60515.

2. Jonathan Edwards, "A Faithful Narrative of a Surprising Work of God," in *The Works of Jonathan Edwards,* vol. 1 (Edinburgh: Banner of Turth, 1974), 354.

3. I am indebted to Dr. John White for these ideas. See John White, *When the Spirit Comes,* 60–61.

Chapter 10
A Biblical Case for Healing

1. C. Everett Koop, "Faith-Healing and the Sovereignty of God," in *The Agony of Deceit,* ed. Michael Horton (Chicago: Moody Press, 1990), 169. Copyright 1990, Moody Bible Institue of Chicago. Used by permission.

2. Ibid., 173–74.

3. Ibid., 176–77.

Chapter 11
When the Spirit Brings a Slow Recovery

1. Winston S. Churchill, "Painting as a Pastime," reprinted with the permission of Charles Scribner's Sons, an imprint of Macmillan Publishing Company from AMID THESE STORMS by Winston Churchill. Copyright 1932 Charles Scribner's Sons; copyright renewed © 1960 Winston S. Churchill.

2. Archibald Thomas Robertson, *The Acts of the Apostles,* vol. 3. of *Word Pictures in the New Testament* (Nashville, Tenn.: Broadman Press, 1930), 480.

3. Charles F. Pfeiffer and Everett F. Harrison, eds., *The Wycliffe Bible Commentary* (Chicago: Moody Press, 1962), 1176.

4. Taken from Eugene H. Peterson, *A Long Obedience in the Same Direction* (Downers Grove, Ill.: InterVarsity Press, 1980), 102, 103. Used by permission of InterVarsity Press, P.O. Box 1400, Downers Grove, Ill. 60515.

5. C. S. Lewis, *The Problem of Pain* (New York: Macmillan, 1962), 93.

Chapter 12
Power, Power . . . We've Got the Power!

1. A. W. Tozer, *The Knowledge of the Holy* (New York: Harper & Brothers, 1961), 16–17.

Chapter 13
Is That All There Is to the Spirit's Ministry?

1. Taken from Stuart Hample and Eric Marshall, comps., *Children's Letters to God* (New York: Workman Publishing, 1991), 6, 7, 9, 11, 14, 17, 21, 26, 44.
2. Ibid., 49.
3. A personal letter. Used by permission.
4. Charles Haddon Spurgeon, *Spurgeon's Morning and Evening* (Grand Rapids, Mich.: Zondervan, 1965), 95.